arise
DAUGHTER

arise DAUGHTER

FINDING YOUR IDENTITY
THROUGH FAITH AND COMMUNITY

PEARL FLORES

Arise Daughter
FINDING YOUR IDENTITY THROUGH FAITH AND COMMUNITY
By Pearl Flores

Copyright © 2022 Pearl Flores. All rights reserved. Except for brief quotations for review purposes, no part of this book may be reproduced in any form without prior written permission from the author.

Scripture quotations marked NIV are taken from the *Holy Bible, New International Version*®, NIV® Copyright ©1973, 1978, 1984, 2011 by Biblical, Inc.® Used by permission. All rights reserved worldwide.

Scriptures quotations marked NKJV are taken from the *Holy Bible New King James Version*®. Copyright © 1982 by Thomas Nelson. Used by permission. All rights reserved.

Scripture quotations marked NASB are taken from the *Holy Bible, New American Standard Bible*®, Copyright © 1960, 1971, 1977, 1995, 2020 by The Lockman Foundation. All rights reserved.

Scripture quotations marked TBT are taken from the *Holy Bible, The Passion Translation*®. Copyright © 2017, 2018, 2020 by Passion & Fire Ministries, Inc.

Used by permission. All rights reserved. thePassionTranslation.com

Cover design and book layout by PearCreative.ca

To contact the author: info@pearlflores.com

ISBN (Print): 979-8-418018-69-4

If you can't feed a hundred, feed one.
MOTHER TERESA

———————————

To you, Jeremy Lane, forever and a day.

Bug, this book is for you.
You are the little boy who entered my life and helped my heart heal. You are also the little boy who left my life and helped me find my faith again. I will always love you, son.

CONTENTS

A NOTE FROM THE AUTHOR	1
INTRODUCTION	3

PART ONE | FINDING HEALING

1.	GROWING PAINS	9
2.	HERE I AM	21
3.	THE PREDATOR	31
4.	SELF DESTRUCTION	39
5.	SCRIBBLE	47

PART TWO | FINDING TRUTH

6.	FORGIVENESS IS FOR ME	59
7.	RE-FIRED	67
8.	AT ARM'S LENGTH	75
9.	ISOLATION	83
10.	KINDRED SPIRITS	91

PART THREE | FINDING RESTORATION

11.	SHELTERED SAFE	101
12.	A WALK WITH GOD	109
13.	CLAIMING MY INHERITANCE	117
14.	GOD OF RESTORATION	127

CLOSING DECLARATION	137
APPENDIX A	RESOURCES	139
APPENDIX B	LOSS HISTORY GRAPH	143
APPENDIX C	RELATIONSHIP GRAPH	145
APPENDIX D	RECOVERY COMPONENTS	147

APPENDIX E	FORGIVENESS LETTER TO MR. POPULAR	151
APPENDIX F	FORGIVENESS LETTER TO MYSELF	155
ACKNOWLEDGMENTS		159
ABOUT THE AUTHOR		161

A NOTE FROM THE AUTHOR

This book may provoke uncomfortable emotions for some with its content on child abuse, sexual assault, rape and suicide. If it does, please know you are not alone and that there are people praying for you for healing, restoration and peace.

This is my story, I don't regret any part of it because it has made me who I am today. I don't wish my story on others, but I don't regret it. The people I've touched shoulders with in my life's path I don't hate, despise, or wish evil upon. I wish them all the happiness, love and joy that I have in my life. I tell my story with no ill-intent. Those who are a part of the story on these pages, I pray will come to know God heals, saves and delivers. There are always two sides of every story. This is mine.

INTRODUCTION

I have lived with a secret for most of my life. I was embarrassed by this secret. It was so powerful it had the ability to break me. In fact, for years it did. It would crash like the sea upon my shore breaking me down with every wave. For years this secret wrapped its tentacles around my life, causing me to believe every deceptive thought and feeling. For years it would pull me into the depths of its waters; teasing me with glimmers of hope only to dash hope away with every shipwreck hidden beneath the surface. What was my secret? I believed that I was unworthy. Unworthy of love. Unworthy of happiness. Unworthy to have a family. Unworthy to be whole. Unworthy of it all.

I spent years living under the power of this secret like a scarlet letter on my chest. I was living a life believing I had to conform to what I thought others needed me to be, what I thought they wanted me to be, in hopes of feeling accepted, loved and wanted. I tried to please everyone. My secret caused me to spend years of my life not knowing who I really was, and fighting God about who He said I was. This secret dug deep roots into my psyche, like the deep roots of a shepherd's tree, causing severe depression and anxiety for most of my adult life. That was, until I started on the journey that would change my life forever.

This book is the story of the journey that broke the shackles that bound me. The words that flow here are the words that yearn to be uncovered. I spent years purposely living out the expectations I felt others had for me. I pushed people away in hopes that fewer people would mean fewer expectations and less pretending. I didn't realize that wasn't how life was supposed to be. I'm sharing my journey through trauma, mental illness and self-hatred in order to bring hope, healing and community. I was tired of my secret. Tired of allowing my past to dictate who I was supposed to be. Tired of feeling I was somehow broken, which I had spent most of my life believing. This is my journey through that struggle. My journey, through the belief that because I was anxious and depressed, because I had trauma in my life; that I wouldn't amount to anything. That I didn't deserve to. That I was not worthy of all the good this life has to offer. This is my journey to opening myself up to my community and how that changed everything for me. This is my journey of faith, even when I didn't think I had any, that kept me going, ultimately healing me and helping me become whole.

I am sharing my story with you in hopes that this book will change someone's life. I hope that anyone who has shared my experiences in **any part** of this book reads my story and realizes that they are stronger than the storm, even if it doesn't feel like it. I share my journey with you so you know that you are not alone; you can endure and prevail.

> This book will show you that there is power in not keeping things hidden—from yourself or the world.

There is power in healing. There is power in community. And through Christ you can have both.

part one

FINDING HEALING

chapter one

GROWING PAINS

I can remember the first time like it was yesterday. Although not the events that led up to it. It was a normal balmy day in Hawaii. I was just a kid doing all the kid things. Until suddenly, I was on the floor of my room, balled up in a fetal position, wishing the legs and arms of the woman who should be protecting me would stop making contact with my body.

I was in the 5th or 6th grade. I was happy. My family dynamic was different because my parents were separated, but there was nothing that caused me to worry about who I was, who people thought I was or what life was all about. I had not experienced depression. I had not experienced anxiety. For the most part, I was a happy little Hawaiian girl living her best life. I was oblivious to trauma. I would even venture to say naïve about it. I didn't know, until many years later, how that day would change my life.

I spent most of the last twenty years in and out of therapy. I honestly hate talking about my problems, because that requires showing vulnerability. But, mostly because I'm ashamed of it. I also feel like a huge burden to the poor soul that has to sit there and listen to my very emotionally charged psyche (even if I pay them). Even though I absolutely hate talking about my problems, I have found therapy, well, therapeutic. I have been fortunate enough to meet some great therapists who have helped me on my journey. I have had some not so great therapists as well and, in a sense, they have helped me through life too. I couldn't have gone through my baggage, my life, without every single one of them.

During a recent therapy session, I was asked, "If there was one thing in your past that you could point your finger at as the start of your depression, could you? Could you name it?"

As I sat there thinking about her question I began to fidget with my rings. I could feel the anxiety rising in me. "I mean," I glance at her quickly then back down to my feet, "I could, but what would be the point of that?"

Here's the thing about me, while I have grown quite a bit in accepting the person that I am today, I still struggle greatly with the shame of my past. I have made a lot of mistakes that contributed to some messed up things. Not everything was my fault, but I have carried the weight of every mistake done by everyone in my life squarely on my shoulders. In my head I thought, "I could have been a better person, a better daughter, a better sister, a better wife, a better mother, a better friend. I could have loved more, forgiven more, accepted more." I have learned that I can't control other's actions or thoughts. What I can control are my own. But, old habits die hard. Some days I still get caught up in the "what ifs". What if I had been a better person at this certain point of my life? Then maybe this certain circumstance would not have happened?

My therapist waited until I looked up at her again and she smiled the "you pay me to dredge up your past so stop being stubborn" smile and said, "We have to acknowledge the past to be able to live in the present."

Gut check.

I sat there shaking in my boots because truth be told I didn't need to think hard on where I needed to point that finger. The moment she asked me the question my mind immediately drifted back to that night when my mom couldn't control her temper and found me to take it out on. I knew immediately I would now have to tell her about that day. I would have to bring up parts of my past I would rather soon forget. Wasn't I here just to get help with the immense grief of losing my foster dad and my foster son? I mean, that is why I called her on that rainy day in April, almost unable to take a breath through my grief. And still, she sat there waiting patiently as my brain raced trying to figure out what to tell her. Those who know me well know to never push me to talk until I am ready. She was one of those people.

"Do you want to tell me about it?" So much for waiting patiently and not being pushy.

The weight of her question quickened my heart. With anxiety thumping in my ears I uttered, "Well, not really, but I guess if this is what brings healing." While my words oozed with sarcasm, I really wanted healing. I have spent most of my life looking for healing. I knew without a doubt she was right, and I needed to put my big girl pants on and be honest with myself and others for once in my life.

> We have to acknowledge the past to be able to live in the present.

In twenty years of therapy I had never brought up this memory. Likely the reason I had never been able to fight through the depression and anxiety that had hit me like tidal waves since I was a kid. "Here I go," I thought. I remember physically taking a deep breath as I attempted to steady my beating heart and begin to tell her about the first time I was physically abused.

I can only remember the moment I lay on the ground wishing to be anywhere but where I was. I wish I could remember what led up to those events. Did I get in trouble at school? Did I sass my mom? Was I caught doing something I wasn't supposed to be doing? I don't know. I have always felt different than my family. I have always felt like I was the one that chose to not be covered under the family "umbrella," not falling in line and conforming to the person that my family wanted me to be. I would talk back when I didn't agree with them. I would choose one direction when they chose to go a different direction. This caused a lot of friction in our home. Friction that made it entirely possible that I had done any or all of those things that day. I was a pretty ornery kid.

I have always wanted to ask my family about that night but have been unable to. In my culture an incident like this is taboo to talk about. It is also considered disrespectful to my family to talk to others about it. In my culture anyone who talks about such things is looked at as someone who has brought shame to their family. Therefore, incidents like these stay "where they belong," in the past, in a cave, with huge rocks and moss covering the entry as if nothing lay behind it. That is where all the wrong my family members have deemed I have ever done and that we have never talked about resides. Our culture is a proud culture, our family (past and present generations) are a proud family and our unwritten rule is we do not bring shame to our family, no matter the cost. My mouth had felt like it was sewn shut for years. When I looked up at my therapist, I knew, suddenly, it was not.

The ground was hard and cold. The floor of the room I shared with my cousin and sister was like the floors in a 1990s classroom: rock solid and devoid of life. That is what pushed up against me as I took the unleashed anger of my mom. I covered my head in hopes that I wouldn't feel my head bounce off the concrete floor when I was hit once again. I don't remember how long it lasted. I can't tell you of any pain I felt. I don't remember it. I only remember how the movements of my body and my mom's arms and legs moved in sync, as if this was a choreographed scene in a production play. The beating couldn't have lasted very long. But, it was loud enough for our neighbor, who lived right above us, to knock on our front door. My mom answered and said we were fine. We were, weren't we? We were always "fine." Our family has been able to get through some pretty rough circumstances and we were always "fine." We were, after all, family. We stuck together through thick or thin, we had each other's backs. That was who we were.

That night when my mom left the room to answer the door, I refused to leave the room. I didn't even move. I didn't dare. I was too embarrassed to show my face. Plus, I knew I somehow deserved it. Even if I can't remember what I did, I truly felt I deserved it. I was already a disgrace and I wasn't going to shame my family any more by gracing the shadows of our front door with my presence.

I don't remember much that happened immediately after the incident. The next thing I recall, I was standing in the apartment parking lot, looking at my dad. Mom had called him to pick me up because she couldn't look at me anymore. I remember my dad telling me that

I had made my mom really angry, that she was still angry so I would be sleeping at his place so she could calm down. I can't remember him asking if I was okay. But he must have, right? After all, he was my dad. I was his "Hun Girl," his baby girl. I couldn't fathom him not asking. My dad told me to stay by the car as he went into the apartment to talk to my mom. When he left, I had never felt more alone in my life. I couldn't cry because we didn't cry in our family. That was a sign of weakness. My dad's favorite saying: No pain, No gain. What did I have to gain through all of this pain? I don't know. But, we were a proud Hawaiian Filipino family and weakness was not part of who we were. So, I stood there shaking and ashamed.

I didn't see or hear her coming but before I knew it the neighbor who knocked on our door stood in front of me. She pointed to my ear and said, "Your ear is bleeding." She raised her hand toward my face and instinctively I flinched and put my hand on my ear. She was right. Blood slowly trickled out of my left ear. "Why? How?" I thought to myself. My ear didn't hurt. Why was there blood? She asked her daughter to fetch her a Q-tip and she cleaned up the blood. She stayed outside with me that night until my dad came back out. She didn't ask the obvious questions but her presence there made me feel as if I wasn't as alone as I thought. When my dad was ready to leave, she hugged me and told me I could call her whenever I needed to. As my dad drove us back to his childhood home, farther and farther away from my neighbor, I could feel the loneliness creep in. As we drove away the only thing I could think was, "How do I call you when I don't know your number?"

I looked up at my therapist with that single thought as hot tears rolled down my cheeks. I looked at the clock and realized I still had time left in the session. "Crap," I thought. I did everything I could to not meet her eyes. I felt raw and vulnerable sharing this memory with her. What I really wanted was to get out of there and pretend the last forty minutes never happened. I finally looked up at her once again taking another deep breath, "I didn't have to think hard. As soon as you asked the question my brain took me back to that day. The first day I ever felt alone and abandoned by the people who loved me." Tears began to flow like a waterfall down my cheeks. "I already knew," I whispered.

She gently placed the box of tissues closer to me. "This may be a little hard, but we can do it together. We are going to make a list of your feelings that night."

As I grew older and thought of what kind of mother I wanted to be, I knew without a doubt in my mind what I wanted was to be a mother who let my children know that they were wanted, cherished, loved. My children would know that I make mistakes, but that I will own up to them, ask for forgiveness and accept forgiveness as well. My children would know home was a safe place, always a safe place even through the ups and downs of life. Most of all, my children would know that mom and dad would always be there for them, even when they were wrong, we would love them and get them through it. As I sat in my session that day, anxious to name the feelings from that night, I knew everything I wanted my children to feel in my home was not what I had felt that night and every day since. Looking back, I can see that my parents, my family (immediate and extended) loved me in their own ways, which were the only ways they knew how. But, that kind of hard love was not the kind of love I wanted in my life.

I took another deep breath. She wanted a list? I looked up at her again and began my list.

- Unworthy
- Unloved
- Alone
- A failure

- Scared
- Angry
- Ashamed
- Embarrassed
- Guilty

"That was easy," I tried to smile doing everything I could to calm my heart. I was beginning to feel uncomfortable again, too vulnerable. I didn't want this particular wall of protection I had built up for years to come down. I felt safe but I did not want to have to face the emotions that accompanied the memory of all this.

I explained to her that after the night I was abused I have always felt like the black sheep of the family. No one has said a word to me in over twenty-five years about that night. No one will ever say a word. No one will say a word about how my sisters, brother, cousins and my mom's boyfriend just stood there watching as I was hit over and over again until the knocking on the door stopped it. No one dares to say a word about how I was kicked out to stay with my dad until things calmed down. No one questioned why she was so angry with me in the first place. The hardest thing to face from that night wasn't the fact that I was physically abused. No. The hardest thing to face about that night was the realization that home wasn't safe, my family wouldn't protect me, and I was utterly alone. I was led to believe, I was the sole cause of the dysfunction in my family even if that dysfunction had begun years earlier when we returned to Hawaii.

chapter two

HERE I AM

If you told me the day of my abuse that I'd end up in my dad's car that night heading to his place because my mom couldn't keep her hands to herself, I'd have laughed at you. I would never have thought anything like that could or would ever happen to me. I mean, from what I could remember we were a loving family, I had two parents, a safe and stable home life. I was happy. But, that's the thing about child abuse—or abuse in general. It can happen to anyone. Child abuse can happen in families regardless of social status, the size of their home, the happiness of their family, what part of town they live in, and whether or not they go to church.

> **Child abuse holds no partiality.**

As to why it happens? In my case, I can only speculate. I know that my mom was dealing with marital conflicts (the separation of my parents), stress (raising six kids by herself) and health issues (my sister had been diagnosed with systemic lupus). Or, maybe I triggered something from her past that freaked her out and made her react. I am not condoning or making excuses for her actions, it was wrong no matter what reasons lay behind it. Yet, even still, I know that there is a plethora of reasons a child is harmed the way I was that day. I may never really know why I had to walk that path, but, I do know that hurting people hurt people. Undoubtedly, my mom was hurting.

When people are faced with a trauma such as being abused as a child—whether once or repeatedly—it does something to us physically, mentally and emotionally. It is natural for depression to hit when we feel as alone and helpless as I did the night I was abused.

This life event was the first of many that contributed to my depression and anxiety and played a role in my hatred of myself. Depression though was the driving force of my self-hatred. I can give all of the statistics of depression. I can say, according to the National Institute of Mental Health, in 2017 there was an estimated 17.3 million adults in the US who suffered with one major depressive episode.[1] And according to WHO (World Health Organization), there are over 264 million people who suffer from depression itself.[2] I can explain the different types of depression and anxiety, different treatments and managements. I can go into detail of all the things you would clinically hear about depression. I have heard them all. I spent most of my teenage years and all of my adult life in therapy listening to them. "You need medication. You need to face what scares you. You need more medication. It's a chemical imbalance." All of these could have been true.

> But, for me, depression was a heart imbalance most of all.

When depression has made us hit rock bottom, when the darkness has taken hold and there is nothing left, there really is only one thing we can do: look up.

---

[1] "Depression," National Institute of Mental Health, https://www.nimh.nih.gov/health/topics/depression, accessed August 2021

[2] "Depression," World Health Organization, https://www.who.int/news-room/fact-sheets/detail/depression, accessed August 2021

It took me a long time to be able to look up to Jesus. It took me over twenty years after being physically abused to give in and look up into the face of Jesus. I had to first understand what all of my feelings meant. I had to understand what trauma was and what it meant to me personally. I had to learn that after my traumatic experience it was normal for me to feel unsafe in myself and unsafe in the world. Before I was willing to look into the face of Jesus, I had to first accept the fact that trauma was present.

According to the American Psychological Association, "Trauma is an emotional response to a terrible event like an accident, rape or natural disaster."[3] The trauma does not have to directly happen to you. It can happen to a family member, a friend, someone you know or don't know. It is an event that causes harm in all ways: mentally, physically, emotionally and spiritually.

In all my years of therapy I never talked about that night and the trauma I pushed down. We focused on other parts of my past—like when my stepdad was killed by a drunk driver or when I was put into the foster care system as a teenager. I didn't see the physical abuse as trauma. I didn't see how that night shaped

---

3 "Trauma," American Psychological Association, https://www.apa.org/topics/trauma, accessed August 2021

the person I had become five, ten and twenty years later. Subconsciously I had done everything I could to repress what had happened that night. As other things began to happen in my life the trauma mounted. Each trauma of my past sat on my chest, as heavy as an elephant, pushing the child abuse down until I didn't even see it anymore. That is, until the weight of my past caught up to me.

You see trauma isn't a one size fits all, where you know what to "expect," a cookie cutter sort of thing. Everyone deals with it differently, because it effects each person differently. Trauma can cause emotional responses like depression and anxiety. It can cause fears and feelings of helplessness. Trauma can cause physical responses such as tight muscles, tightness in the chest and difficulty breathing and other physical diseases and immune disorders. Lack of concentration and memory loss or the inability to problem solve are trauma induced cognitive responses. Behavioral responses to trauma include angry outbursts, difficulty sleeping, suicidal ideation and substance abuse. Not being able to recognize our trauma causes our quality of life to be diminished. Not being able to process our trauma will cause us to continually feel a sense of fear, isolation and hopelessness.

When I sought Jesus and was willing to say I had trauma in my life restoration began in me. I had to realize that the trauma I endured wasn't because I was broken or dysfunctional or a really bad daughter. Trauma happens because sometimes terrible things happen to good people. In order for me to begin healing I had to stop pretending nothing had happened. I had to stop pushing it deep down into the cellar of my soul. I had to recognize it and let it breathe because trying to suffocate it was doing more damage than good.

Which is why finding our identity in Christ starts with acknowledging our trauma. How can we expect to heal when we can't face head on the fact that something negative or traumatic happened to us? That doesn't mean we have to relive our trauma and every single detail to the point we feel we're drowning. It just means we look at the trauma and work through it, so it no longer defines us, no longer controls us and no longer suffocates us and robs us of the physical air we breathe.

> Allow God the chance to take your deepest, darkest pain and blossom it into the most extraordinary rose to ever bloom.

Acknowledging and owning our trauma isn't easy. There is no "one stop shop" fix. Rome wasn't built in a day.

Neither is healing from the pains of physical, emotional or mental abuse recovered in a single moment. As we face our trauma, as we snuff the brooding fire it has built within us, it's important to equip ourselves with some coping skills. Coping skills are important because they can help us through the moments we feel triggered.

Here are some of my favorite coping skills:

The Winchester

The official name is Containment but that doesn't motivate or encourage me. It made me feel stifled. So, I renamed it. Using imagery, we create a box where we put anything in our life that upsets and triggers us. It doesn't have to only be our trauma either. When my husband annoys me and I can't deal with it, it goes in the box. As we begin to feel triggered or out of sorts, we can contain our issue until we feel better grounded. My box is a Tungsten steel black trunk with padlocks placed in the middle of a glass room inside of a larger room. If something triggers me I unlock the padlocks, put those triggers in there, seal it shut and walk out of those rooms. This allows me to gather myself and when I am ready I can slowly pull out the trigger, or issue, and confront it.

The Happy Place

Like the Winchester, this coping skill uses imagery. Imagery is a pretty powerful tool. The Happy Place technique uses our imagination to take us to our favorite place, a place that calms us. Mine is a white sandy beach in my hometown. Taking a deep breath, we use all our senses to be there. What do I see? What do I hear? What do I smell? What do I feel? We bring ourselves to a place where we are calm and relaxed. We can stay as long as we like. In our Happy Place the world is our oyster.

Butterfly Hugs

This is a calming/breathing technique. Place your arms crisscross over your chest as if you are hugging yourself. Taking a deep breath, tap your fingers on your shoulder as fast or as slow as you like. Breathe in. Breathe out. Focus on controlling your breathing. Being able to control your breathing allows your body's fight or flight reaction to calm.

Using these coping skills, or ones that work best for us, helps us to understand, tolerate and confront our trauma which in turn helps us along the path to being the best version of ourselves we can be. Understanding our trauma brings healing for ourselves and others.

Look, there isn't a magic wand in facing our trauma. There isn't a quick fix out there. It really isn't going to be easy. It isn't going to be pretty. There may be a heck of a lot of ugly crying but, the end result is worth it. I spent so much time denying the hurt caused by my family and hiding the pain those memories triggered. But, when I could look my trauma in the eye, when I could say, "You do not define me," it was then that I could accept and forgive my parents for the pain in my childhood. When I could look my trauma in the eye and not allow it to control me, restoration began. It was then I could say, "God, here I am, feeling broken, and asking You to pour into me. Pour the gold of Your love, grace and mercy into my life so that everything broken is made new." When I began to stop pushing the trauma down pretending it never happened, when I began to call it by its name, I could hear God say, "Here I am."

chapter three

THE PREDATOR

We read it in books that have an ounce of romance. Or we watch it on our favorite tv series. A girl gets swept off her feet by the jock who is charismatic, a looker and everyone's friend. It happened to me, too. He was Mr. Popular. He played basketball and baseball. He looked good in his uniforms. He knew all the right things to say. And, boy was he a charmer! He did all the right things to put those butterflies in my stomach. He quite easily and quickly swept me off my feet. Mr. Popular made me laugh. He made me feel less alone. He made me feel wanted. He made me laugh. He made me feel special.

When we started dating, I was pleasantly surprised to discover our parents had grown up together. He and his family lived two streets above us, which made it pretty convenient for us to see each other. We spent most of our time hanging out in school and during basketball practice. He even asked me to our class dance. It almost felt like a fairy tale. I felt like he really got me. For a girl who was struggling with self-esteem issues having someone look at me the way he did, someone who listened to every word I said, someone who understood me, it felt like a good thing.

When we started dating, I had amazing grades. As a part of the "sporty" popular kids, I did stupid things, both on and off campus, but I had my head on straight. I planned to graduate with honors, work my butt off at practice and become a pro basketball player. In my head, because of my small size, I was going to be an amazing 3 and D player who left her heart on the floor every single night. I may not have been the best or even a little gifted of a basketball player, but my grit and passion for the game would be my ticket off the rock where I lived on to a life I had always wanted. The easy on the eyes boyfriend was the cherry on top of the cake. I thought nothing could go wrong.

One summer we both attended summer school. On the last day of summer school, we decided he would hang out at my place for a little bit. We had rules in our house—no boys allowed alone in our rooms. If a boy was in our room someone else needed to be in there and the door needed to stay open. No one was home but at this point in our relationship I had no reason to believe anything outside of a make out session would happen. I don't think I could have been any more naïve than I was that day.

I can still feel the emotion and shock of what happened like it was yesterday.

My family was in the midst of moving so we went to my parents' room where the only TV was. I sat on the bed and he got comfortable beside me. We channel surfed for a bit talking about what we'd do the rest of the summer. Then we started making out. His hands would travel and I had no problem bringing them back to my waist each time they did. Even then, I still felt safe. I believed he respected me. I kept telling myself we both know the limits. As he continued to move his hands in areas that were not welcomed my heart began beating erratically. I thought, "What the hell am I doing? What is going on? What is he doing?" Thoughts flew through my head as I began to become more and more uncomfortable. "Please, stop."

"Babe, it's gonna be okay."

I remember everything that happened in those next few minutes in complete and accurate detail. I remember how I felt, what I thought. But instead of fighting, I froze. I should have fought. My dad had taught me to fight. I could have fought. But, I froze, trembling in terror, a cold shiver running down my back. I couldn't catch my breath. There was a power to him that I never knew was there and no matter how much I struggled I barely moved an inch under his strength. My life flashed before my eyes. I begged God to let it be over.

When it was over I didn't know whether to move or stay put. I could hear his quickened breathing next to me. I could feel my body shaking. I was cold, so very cold. I didn't have the strength to move, or to even open my eyes. I couldn't look at him. I heard him stand up and put his clothes back on. I never imagined this would ever happen. How could he have done this to me? I thought he loved me. I closed my eyes and waited. I could hear him put on his shirt, wrap his belt around his waist and slip on his shoes. I waited and listened as I counted every footstep he took. One, two, three, four, five, six, seven, eight, nine. He stopped and the hammering in my chest quickened. I was afraid he would return to the room. Then I heard the front door open and click shut behind him.

I felt like roadkill. I felt like a raccoon who wasn't fast enough to get to the other side of the street. I lay lifeless on the road, with cars passing me by like I never mattered. I felt mangled, like I had bled out, having been hit by a driver who carelessly goes on with their life. I continued lying there, without the strength to move. I was frozen in place and afraid that he would return. How long did I have before he came back for me? And when he returned, how long did I have before he became angry and what would happen then? How long did I have before I saw those cold steel eyes burning into me again asking for more than he had already taken? I had to get up. I couldn't risk anyone seeing me like this. What would my mom say if she knew? What would my dad do if I let the pain control me? I was brought up to be strong headed and stubborn. I had to get up.

I felt for my shirt and underwear. My hand shook as I tried to gather the energy to put them on. Struggling, I didn't even bother. I slowly found the strength to stand. My parent's bathroom was just a few feet away. I took a deep breath, telling myself it was my fault for leading him on and found the energy to head through the bathroom door. Dropping my clothes on the floor I turned the shower on as I watched the blood wash down the drain. I sat in that shower until the burning water turned as cold as the Arctic sea.

You may have heard about Post Traumatic Stress Disorder with soldiers who come back from fighting a war. When we have to fight for our life and take the lives of others it isn't a surprise that we would return home with PTSD. I can't imagine how that would feel. What I didn't know was that PTSD wasn't only for war vets. It was also for people like me who suffered a traumatic experience. According to Dr. Dean G. Kilpatrick, "Almost one-third (31%) of all rape victims developed PTSD sometime during their lifetime."[4] One. Third. As a lonely scared teenager, I was suffering from a disorder that felt like a monster hovering in the shadows slowly causing my psyche to be destroyed from the inside out.

Being raped changed me into someone unrecognizable. The girl that stared back at me was not the girl I remember. I felt numb. The plans I had for my future didn't mean anything to me anymore. In class I would put on a smile, or sometimes just keep my head down. I would do anything to not draw attention to myself. I didn't want people to see that I was dying inside. I told myself no one would understand, so I remained silent. Before I knew it, my grades began to slip, severely. I went from an honor roll student to a student that was barely

---

4 The Mental Health Impact of Rape," Dean G. Kilpatrick, https://mainweb-v.musc.edu/vawprevention/research/mentalimpact.shtml, accessed September 2021

passing. In my brain there was no life after what he had done to me. I was afraid to live, and yet I was feeding off of this fear. I needed it to breathe, to function even. This fear is what kept me going, pushing me deeper and deeper into denial that anything actually happened.

I told myself it was okay to isolate and seclude myself because that way I'd be safe. No one could hurt me like that again. What I didn't realize was that hiding away in a bedroom was a huge detriment to my healing. Secluding myself from my family caused unspoken suffering for us all. Secluding myself from the world created a mentality in me that if I built high enough walls around my heart, my psyche, my life would be safe.

> Secluding myself put me in darkness so thick and black I could hardly breathe.

I thought that if I built up higher walls around my heart, they would keep the darkness at bay. Instead, it caused the darkness to become darker, engulfing me and saturating every part of me—my heart, my mind, my soul.

Note: If you have ever been sexually assaulted, I want you to know, sweet sister or brother, that I stand beside you. Survivors tend to feel shame and embarrassment.

We often think it was our fault that it happened. We think that we could have done something to stop it. That maybe we should have said, "No" louder, or simply said, "No" instead of freezing. Listen, we like to minimize the experience in hopes to either act like it never happened, or to pretend what happened wasn't a big thing. But, it was. It is. What Mr. Popular did to me was wrong, and what that person did to you was wrong. Stop telling yourself that maybe you should have fought more, or shouldn't have worn that certain outfit, or given the person the wrong idea. No matter where your life path was at that moment, you, dear friend, deserved the utmost respect. You did not deserve to be violated.

If you have been sexually assaulted (no matter how long ago it was) and are seeking help or would like more information, there are people who can and will walk alongside you for healing and restoration. You can call the toll-free number for the Rape, Abuse & Incest National Network (RAINN) at 1-800-656-HOPE. You can also go to their website at hotline.rainn.org/online. Additional resources can be found in Appendix A. Other survivors are here. You are not alone.

chapter four

SELF DESTRUCTION

So much of my life had become dark after the loss of my innocence. In my brain there was no life after what Mr. Popular had done to me. What had happened was a secret I had to guard with my life, and if I was to stand guard over these secrets, I had no time to live. Sadly, refusing to reach out for help only caused me to spiral even further down this deep, dark pit that I had no idea how to climb out of. There was only one way out: I had to find a way to release the darkness.

I convinced myself I needed to let the darkness out without anyone knowing. I was sure there was a way because I couldn't bring myself to burden anyone else with what was going on. I didn't want anyone else to hurt the way I had been hurting. I quickly found that quietly throwing up my food gave me a sense of control in my life. The first time I did that, there was a flood of tears. I mistakenly thought that those tears signified the beginning of my healing, and for the first time I felt a relief, of sorts, for what had happened. As alone and abandoned as I felt, relief set in as I flushed the contents of my stomach down the toilet.

While throwing my food up gave me some comfort, I still felt dead inside. I'd often wake up in a sweat, my mind going back to the day of my assault. Sometimes I'd wake up crying, heart pounding because even in slumber my subconscious would relive that awful day. Some nights I would dream I was in my parents' room again. Other nights I was in public as he caught me and did what he wanted to do. No matter how hard I tried to run from him in my dreams he was always there tormenting me. What was even worse were the dreams where he wasn't alone. In some dreams my family watched. In some dreams a stranger did. In some dreams there were multiples of him, slowly killing my soul.

Meanwhile, the darkness I felt was temporarily being expelled down a toilet. The more I threw up my food, the more I began to realize the darkness never really went away. It hovered above my head high enough where I couldn't see it, like a black cloud growing darker and darker billowing overhead larger and larger. Until, unaware the cloud slowly descended into my atmosphere, ever so slowly, surrounding me with piercing darkness that suffocated me until the cycle would start all over again. Every single day I'd sit in silent agony, trying to find a way to, once and for all, get rid of the storm inside.

I remember how my next fix started. I was in the kitchen cutting some fruit for a beach day with my family. The knife slipped; my finger was in the wrong place. *Slice.* I pulled back in shock as blood dripped steadily down my finger. My finger throbbed as I ran it under the water. That's when I noticed the pain in my heart wasn't there. It was focused on the cut on my finger. How did that work? How did I not know emotional torment could be taken away by physical pain?

It took me awhile to get the "courage" to slice my finger again. When I did the pain instantly transferred from my heart to my finger. Every few days I'd cut open the same wound watching the blood drip enjoying every second of physical pain. Soon enough though, I realized I was doing it wrong. My finger needed to heal to prevent inquisitive minds from knowing. So, I became determined to be more secretive. I moved it where I knew clothing would cover it—my stomach, my thighs or my shoulder. I realized hiding the cut meant I could do it more often and I did. I took full advantage of the secrecy.

> I was an absolute hot mess express.

My parents knew I wasn't trying in school. I had begun to be defiant and angry. No one would ever understand what was going on. I just knew they'd blame me if they found out. I already blamed myself. I couldn't ask them or anyone else for help. I couldn't understand why my life had to be as it was, but I thought I deserved it. I was sinking deeper into the pit of quicksand that I created, and I could barely breathe. I needed another fix.

The first time I lit my skin on fire wasn't like the first time I cut myself open. I didn't cry, instead I relished in the pain. I told myself I deserved all of the pain. No one loved me, so this pain was good. It made me feel something. Every time I would begin to feel like I was coming undone, I'd press against a burn and feel the heat of pain wash over me. In my brokenness it felt glorious. I even got creative one night. I took out the lighter and began my quest. I'd heat the lighter's cap, place it on my skin and repeat. By the end of it my stomach screamed as red as a bloodstained ruby branded with a "P." My brand stared back at me as if laughing, goading me to keep going. It took about an hour for the burning to subside; when it did, I dug into those blisters to feel it again. Today, I hate to show my stomach because permanently scarred on my right lower abdomen is a "P," a reminder of a life I am so grateful I am no longer trapped in.

I was getting really tired. Tired of hurting, tired of the nightmares, tired of the life that I now lived. I was tired, most of all, of what I was doing to my family. The purging didn't help. The self-mutilation didn't help. I had to make this easier for everyone. I felt there was no other choice. I decided I should kill myself.

Hear me out on this. I didn't decide to kill myself because I was throwing some kind of pity party. I didn't decide to kill myself because I was running away from my problems. I didn't decide to kill myself because I was a coward. I had decided to kill myself because I fully believed that with me out of my family's life it would make their lives infinitely better than it was with me in it. I felt the life I was living was selfish. I wanted to be as selfless as possible to those I loved. I wanted to end my life so no one had to put up with the crap of me anymore.

One day I took a box cutter from my parents' room and took a walk. I had already done research. I knew how to do it. I knew where to cut. I just needed to find the perfect time and the perfect place. I sat myself on a park bench, lifted the blade to my wrist and pierced my skin. I saw a trickle of blood run down my wrist. All the air was sucked out of my body. Something felt off, wrong. I watched that scarlet red liquid drip onto the park bench with a sickness in me. I couldn't figure out what it was. I just knew I had to find the strength to get back up. I threw the box cutter in the garbage and walked home.

I felt irrevocably and utterly broken.

> The depression had dug its tentacles so deeply into my core that I couldn't tell you anymore who I was and who I wasn't.

I couldn't tell you how I felt, because at this point every part of me felt numb. Anger coursed through me every single second of the day. Hatred of my life, and hatred of those who were happy oozed out of my pores. The happy life of a girl who just wanted to play basketball was suddenly a secret life where self-mutilation and suicidal ideations were my norm.

I had begun to blame myself for every bad thing that was happening in my life. The assault? My fault. The depression? My fault. The anxiety? My fault. The lack of friends? My fault. The lack of love from my family?

My fault. The abuse from my mother all those years ago festered in my heart, but I had buried it so deep that all I saw was the claws of Mr. Popular digging for what was left of me. The child abuse and sexual abuse left me alone on an island with no way to call for help. I had burnt every possible piece of equipment I could have used to signal any rescue planes flying overhead simply because I was embarrassed someone would find out and be disappointed.

Note: During this time of my life I was in such despair. I thank God that He protected me from ending my life. I thank God for His saving grace. While I can thank Him now, I couldn't then. It was too dark for me to see what was right in front of me, much less be willing to look up. If you are in a position where your life feels worthless and devoid of meaning, please reach out. Your life holds meaning. Your life holds significance. Your life means more than you can ever know. Don't give up. Reach out. You are not alone. There are people who care deeply about you. Including myself. I will always be here for my readers to lend an ear, say a prayer or just be.

chapter five

SCRIBBLE

"I don't love you."

I was on a different island spending the summer with my best friend, when the call came in. When I knew it was my family I felt a heaviness lift. My teenage psyche was relieved. I knew they had received my letter. I have always been better at writing my emotions than saying them. When I speak, I jumble my words and don't make sense. Or I talk really fast, repeating myself because I had forgotten what I said. With writing, the words have always seemed to come easier. So, when I told my family about the sexual assault I had written a letter. I told them everything. I told them about that day. I told them of my fear of coming home now that I had told people what he had done, of my fear of what he'd do to me now that I had shared our secret. I confessed the eating disorder, self-mutilation, and suicidal ideations. I poured out my heart on those pages. They finally knew. Every secret. Every pain. Every shame. They finally knew about the darkness that had engulfed me and they were calling to check on me. I knew things would be better now that the truth was out.

"Get home now." I didn't understand what was happening. "Get home now so we can talk about this as a family. Get home, so you can tell him to his face what you have told me he did to you." The realization of what was being asked hit me like a battering ram used to break down castle doors. My family was angry because I had just aired dirty laundry that directly affected them. They were angry because, by not bringing this to them privately first I, once again, brought shame to the family. Most of all, they were angry because they didn't believe me.

I broke down. All of my shame slammed against me like a tsunami that wiped out all hope of relief I had anticipated just moments ago. "I can't." I pleaded. "I can't face him."

"You can't accuse him of something and not face him and say it."

I begged and pleaded. I had told them what happened and they still insisted I fly back home. I implored them not to force me to come back home until he was gone, they scoffed at me. They proceeded to tell me that Jeremy's grandfather's church had brainwashed me. My family believed the people in that church were part of a cult that had taught me ungodly things. The church was the reason I was making these accusations. They were the reason I was tearing our family apart. The disdain in my mom's voice was as sharp as a knife and every word cut deeply into the very depths of my soul.

At the end of the call I told them I was sorry. I was sorry for embarrassing them and that I loved them. I heard my mom as clear as day, "I don't love you." Click.

The division that letter caused was only the beginning of further heartbreak for all of us. My refusal to return home caused my family to report me as a runaway. I was picked up by two officers who proceeded to fly me back home. Telling my story found me in front of a judge as I heard my family tell him, "We can't live with her anymore." The sound of the gavel still rings in my ears. That sound emphasized the finality of my family giving up on me, turning their backs and walking away.

Being thrown into foster care was like losing my family through unexpected, sudden death. Suddenly, I was a ward of the state. The heaviest of grief swept over me and became my constant companion.

Everyone will face grief at some point in their life. For me, every time grief came knocking at my door, it didn't just knock. It was the Big Bad Wolf and he came to blow my entire house down. Every time he came knocking, I'd let it destroy me a little more. When the judge hit the gavel against that sound block, it was the final blow. I didn't even try to hold on until the storm passed, instead I let the winds take me. Grief and loss can do that to us. When we experience a loss in our lives our natural reaction is grief. Grief over the memories. Grief over the things that were or weren't said. Grief over what remained unresolved. Grief over the "what could have beens."

When I entered the foster care system all of those aspects of grief rushed over me. And then some. I went through all the stages of grief (denial, anger, bargaining, depression and acceptance), over and over again being caught in a vicious whirlpool. I think sometimes our expectation of grief is that we go from the bottom and we work our way up and out of it. But, it doesn't work like that. Grief really isn't linear. Grief looks more like scribbles, like the pattern of two squirrels running after each other through the trees or like the flight of scattered ducks when a dog plunges through them.

Some days I'd be in denial. My parents loved me. I wasn't in foster care. This was going to be temporary. My parents would come for me soon, then my heart would go numb and I just wouldn't, couldn't feel anything.

There were also the angry days. There were a lot of angry days. Days where I said, "Screw the world!" Days where I hated everyone, whether I knew them or not.

Depression was always there, but it was most prevalent when I felt isolated, abandoned and alone. I'd tell myself that no one loved me. No one wanted me. I wasn't worth the breath of life given to me. Afterwards, I'd get angry all over again. I'd want to run away and avoid all the things in life.

Some days I'd bargain with my brain, if it could just get through this I'd be happier. So, I'd begin to tell my story, opening up little by little in hopes that maybe, just maybe, I'd find someone who could help me out of the muck.

Then I'd get angry again. I really did get angry a lot. Denial, depression, bargaining was always met with even more anger. Anger that no one loved me, anger that no one wanted me, anger that no one thought I was worth even a second of their time. Why did I have to go through this? This wasn't fair. Why me?

I wish I knew then what I know now about grief. I always thought I was broken, that there was something wrong with me. But it was the grief. The crying, the detachment, the insomnia was grief. The anxiety, anger and fatigue were also grief. All of my isolation, my guilt and declining health had grief written all over them. I was grieving the loss of so many things.

> None of us are at our best when we are grieving.

Unresolved grief becomes a stumbling block. Never facing that grief, never accepting that all the loss in my life actually happened, never coming to terms with it caused grief to rewrite my core identity. It gave me a different name, a new place to live, a new attitude and a new job. Grief changed me physically, too. Suddenly I had a new cut, I dressed differently, I talked differently. Grief changed my value system, my attitude and my outlook on life. Each time loss happened grief took a chunk of who I was supposed to be and changed it. I would look in the mirror and not recognize the girl that stared back at me. There was a hollowness in her eyes, devoid of life, and filled with utter hopelessness and sadness.

My plan of graduating high school with honors and attending UC Berkley had become a figment of my imagination. I was just an empty shell, a robot that woke up every day going through the motions and doing what was expected of me. I had lost the spark of life within me. Grief had stolen my identity and I didn't have the strength of heart to steal it back.

I began to question God. Why did He think loving me was even a good idea? Why did He think getting me out of all my trauma was worth it? The more I questioned Him the more tugging on my heart I felt. When I was put into foster care, I didn't have a Bible. So, Jeremy's sister ripped out Psalm 27 out of her Bible and said to hold the declaration close to my heart. As the shadows of darkness continued to engulf me, I kept going back to that chapter out of Psalm.

> When the wicked came against me
> To eat up my flesh,
> My enemies and foes,
> They stumbled and fell.
> Though an army may encamp against me,
> My heart shall not fear;
> Though war may rise against me,

> In this I will be confident.
> For in the time of trouble
> He shall hide me in His pavilion;
> In the secret place of His tabernacle
> He shall hide me;
> He shall set me high upon a rock.
> Do not hide Your face from me;
> Do not turn Your servant away in anger;
> You have been my help;
> Do not leave me nor forsake me,
> O God of my salvation.
> When my father and my mother forsake me,
> Then the Lord will take care of me.
>
> (Psalm 27:2-3, 5, 9-10)

Psalm 27 is a declaration of King David's faith even when there were armies attacking on the left and right of him. Between all of the trauma, I had forgotten who I was. While God knew, He didn't push it. Instead, He declared His faithfulness through a chapter ripped out of a Bible, during the darkened nights of my life.

> **God whispered softly in my ear words of comfort, of promise, of strength.**

He always found ways to remind me of the times He carried me, of the times that He held me tight, of the times He was my refuge.

Grief had stolen who I was. God knew I wasn't ready to allow Him to help me take it back. So, He sent me people, like Jeremy's sister, to help nudge me on the path. You see, I had to come to terms with the fact that no matter what I did, my story never changed. My story, instead, changed me. And it was up to me to stop hiding from my grief, do the hard work, and take control of how my story changed me.

part two

FINDING TRUTH

chapter six

FORGIVENESS IS FOR ME

It has been over two decades since the assault. In those years I have had nightmares, insomnia, eating disorders, depression and anxiety. I have been afraid of the dark, afraid of large and loud crowds, afraid of people getting close. In the beginning I became a person I never thought I would ever be. I hated who I was. I was angry at the world. I thought I deserved everything that happened that day. He was right, I led him on and I had to live with the consequences of my actions.

He said that I was the tease, that I invited him to destroy my body, and for years I believed him. I believed that I wasn't worth a second look. I believed I was unworthy to be loved. I believed that I deserved everything bad that had ever happened in my life. Every. Single. Thing. Every heartache, every pain, every misfortune, every abandonment, I deserved. I deserved it because I was somehow flawed, somehow a horrible person and horrible things should happen to horrible people.

I hated him for years. I hated him for what he did to me. I hated him for making me afraid of every unknown part of my life. I hated him for taking away my joy, for taking away my happiness. I hated him for taking my relationship with my family. I hated him for taking my innocence. No longer did I see the boy that I could play a fun pickup basketball game with. He was the menacing shadow when I turned the corner in the parking lot at night. He was the foreboding presence when I walked down my darkened hallways at three o'clock in the morning. He was the not-so-lookalike man startling me in a lit up grocery aisle, standing a few feet away from me. Most of all, he was the voice in my head laughing and taunting me for years that I was unworthy to be loved.

After what he did, this boy didn't deserve to be forgiven or anything good from me. Yet, Heaven had an entirely different plan. As I continued to heal from my past, I realized I couldn't heal as long as I refused to forgive him for everything he had done to me. I couldn't heal from being afraid of my own shadow. I couldn't heal from being afraid of going into a local store. I couldn't heal from the anxiety that would overtake me every time there was a knock on the door. If I wanted to heal from the darkness and fear that had imprisoned me all these years, I had to forgive the boy that took my innocence. As I grappled with that idea I realized something: forgiveness isn't for the one that hurt me.

> Forgiveness is for me.

Forgiveness is for my healing, my sanity, my freedom. Forgiveness is the key that will unlock the shackles that had become heavy weights around my neck, suffocating me more every single day.

So, I began the process to forgive him.

I had begun reading a book with my therapist called, "The Grief Recovery Handbook" by John W. James and Russell Friedman. If you are going through any type of grief I would highly suggest this book. James and Friedman made walking through my grief (all of my grief, not just the sexual assault) manageable. The book walked me through an exercise I call *Frozen* because it was my chance to let it go. This exercise had four steps:

1. **Create a Loss History Graph**: This graph outlined all of the losses I felt in my life from the time I was born to the present. Nothing was too small to put on the graph. It didn't have to be a deep loss. Every event in my life that caused me some kind of loss I added a tick mark for it. My first loss? The birth of my brother when I was almost four. (See Appendix B)

   There was a shift in my heart when I added events on my timeline. The heaviness began to lift and I could feel the restoration begin working within my heart. Adding each loss, no matter how big or small, became therapeutic. Losses included moving to Seattle as a child, the death of my cousin due to a tragic car accident, and when Jeremy and I were married in 2004 and the only person in my family that attended was my dad. As a visual person, seeing these ticks on my Loss History Graph made it real enough to begin my healing. I cried all the ugly tears creating this graph.

2. **Created a Relationship Graph:** From my Loss History Graph, I chose a relationship that hurt the most and created a graph with tick marks of all the losses on my Loss History Graph that coincided with that relationship. The first time I did this exercise I chose Mr. Popular. Using the Loss History Graph, I was also able to build a relationship graph and complete the *Frozen* exercise for my parents and another person who deeply hurt me. (See Appendix C)

   Ticking my Relationship Graph for Mr. Popular wasn't as hard. The graph ticked every significant thing good or bad in our relationship. So, I included things like the time we first met, when we started dating, the winter ball and when he assaulted me. I also included interactions through the years.

3. **Explored the Recovery Components:** From the Relationship Graph I identified *Amends* (things I needed to make amends for), *Forgiveness* (things I needed to forgive) and *Significant Emotional Statements* also called SES (things I didn't need to amend or forgive but need or want to say). The Amends doesn't mean I did something wrong. I can be sorry for things that were out of

my control, like when we send condolences to a friend who lost a loved one. One of my amends to Mr. Popular was, "I'm sorry I wasn't strong enough to come out earlier." (See Appendix D) When we work through the forgiveness portion it can be hard. It isn't easy to forgive someone who has hurt us. Even if we feel like we are just going through the motions, it is still a powerful exercise. A Pastor friend of mine once said, "Even if you don't believe it purpose in your heart to forgive them. When you do God will work in you to mean it."

Completing the Recovery Components in the *Frozen* exercise felt more of a "going through the motions" sort of thing than the graphs. Mainly because I was still processing all of this. I entered things I asked forgiveness for, wrote down why I forgave him and included any emotional statements that didn't fit in the amends or forgiveness portions. To help clarify SES more, I also wrote things like, "I want you to know that I trusted you and you broke that trust."

4. **Write a Grief Recovery Letter**: This was a letter broken into Amends, Forgiveness and SES—in that order—for the person chosen in Step 2.

Amends are first, so we can ask for forgiveness for the wrong we feel we were responsible for in the relationship. Forgiveness allows us to forgive others for what wrong they took part in. SES allows us to communicate any emotions we feel need to be communicated. Another example of a SES is, "I want you to know, you did not win."

This was a difficult exercise, but when I wrote the Grief Recovery Letter to Mr. Popular I thought of the Cross. I thought of Jesus with a crown of thorns, bleeding from his opened wounds and His skin being ripped apart. I thought of Him looking at me and forgiving me for every stupid and horrible thing I have done. I didn't, and still do not, deserve the sacrifice He gave for my sins. Much like the boy that raped me who I felt didn't deserve my forgiveness for his sins, but, even still. A friend once told me that one of the highest forms of love is intercession for those who have hurt us. As I wept writing the letter, I wept out every ounce of hatred, bitterness and condemnation I had for Mr. Popular. I wrote the letter in the hopes that one day he'd know Jesus. One day he'd ask for the same forgiveness I have. One day he'd know without a doubt that forgiveness was his. Trauma that is not transformed is transmitted. Transmitted into anger. Transmitted into self-hatred. Transmitted into grief. If I wanted to heal from the trauma that Mr. Popular caused I needed to be able to forgive both him and myself. I started with him.

> Trauma that is not transformed is transmitted. Transmitted into anger. Transmitted into self-hatred. Transmitted into grief.

chapter seven

RE-FIRED

For most of my childhood I felt different from my family. I didn't like the things they liked. I didn't act the way they acted. I always felt out of place. I came to understand that those feelings were just a part of my identity crisis. My identity had been crippled by the constant eruption of my life's volcano. Everything I did was to stop the lava flow that threatened and burned down every structure, every bridge and every path I tried to build. The lava flowed every which way, ensuring what I already knew: that I'd become nothing. For a long, long time I believed that.

As I got older, believing the self-hatred and feeling the loneliness made me walk away from God. Why would I serve Him? This was the God that should have protected me from Mr. Popular. This was the God that should have covered me when I was on that hard, cold floor being kicked. This was the God who after all these years of saying He was real suddenly was nowhere to be found when I most needed someone to hold me. This was the God that said He had called me by name. And yet, here I was unnamed.

As I continued to spiral, I began to have the lowest of low self-esteems. I hated the way I looked. My body was too fat, my eyes too big, my ears oddly shaped and my hair too out of control. I hated my voice, my height and the way I walked. I told myself that I didn't deserve happiness. I didn't deserve someone who loved me. I didn't deserve to fulfill any of my dreams. I self-sabotaged every good thing in my life because in my head I didn't deserve happiness. I believed that someone as broken and pathetic as I was had no place being a part of this world.

I was putting a heavy price on my head for things that were out of my control. I didn't ask him to rape me. I didn't ask her to beat me. I didn't ask for any of the bad things that had happened in my life. I didn't do some kind of voodoo magic incorrectly that now I was losing all control. And yet, I continued to break anything that held a chance to fix me. What good could ever come out of someone like me?

As I think back on those dark years I can only shake my head. It is said that we are our biggest critics. Often we find something to hate about ourselves. Our voice. Our height. The way we laugh. There is always something. We forget that in order for us to love others, to understand how to love others we have to first love ourselves. For me that was the hardest thing to do. How could I love myself when others couldn't love me? How could I love myself when I was broken and hit with so much tragedy? How could I love myself when I wasn't worth loving? How could I love myself when others openly admitted they didn't love me?

By forgiving myself.

Our self-worth can be driven by other people's opinions of us. We tend to base our self-worth on what people say and do. We allow them to create a narrative that isn't God-given or God-written. We begin to take what people say about us as truth. Hearing and believing the lies creates anger, guilt and shame. I had bought into the lie. I was the broken toy that needed to be returned to customer service. I was the lemon car driven off the lot. I was a stale batch of french fries served "fresh." I was a failure. I was a fraud. I was my worst enemy; the biggest thing stopping me from being who God created me to be. I had to learn to take those lies and lay them at the feet of Jesus. I had to acknowledge my mistakes and leave them there no matter how much I wanted to just cradle them in my arms because they were my "comfortables." I realized, when I could finally leave all of my tragedy at the feet of Jesus, forgive myself for every lie I believed and everything I actually did wrong, I was able to make peace with the past and move forward.

As I continued to heal from my past God showed me that forgiving myself allowed me to finally love myself for the woman I had become—a woman with faults and failures full of love, compassion and forgiveness. A woman called to help solve the orphan crisis. A woman who is dependable in her job. A woman that loved hard even when she was afraid she'd never be loved back.

I had spent time learning to forgive others for hurting me. Yet, I found forgiving myself was one of the hardest things I have ever done. As I lay my burdens down, I began learning how to forgive myself by doing these things:

1. **I had to be honest with myself.** This meant acknowledging the heaviness I had been carrying and allowing my subconscious to

unpack it, even if some of it had to go into my Winchester (see Chapter 2 "Here I Am", page 18). Acknowledging my feelings meant being completely and totally honest with myself. This meant no more games and no more minimizing my feelings. This meant coming face to face with the anxiety that threatened my existence every time I wanted to be real. Acknowledging my feelings meant that the walls that I had intricately built up HAD to come down.

2. **I had to admit my mistakes and be remorseful.** Too often we use the walls of denial to keep us from being hurt. When we can confront our actions we let the burdens of those actions fall at our feet. I am not perfect. As hard as my past was, as horrible as the things that were done to me were, I still made mistakes. I had to apologize for that. I had to look at the patterns in my life, look at what I was doing to survive instead of heal. I had to confront those patterns. As humans we will make mistakes. Mistakes do not negate the fact that we are worthy to be loved, wanted, cherished and adored. Our mistakes do not determine our worth.

3. **I wrote myself a Grief Recovery letter.** After all, I am in a relationship with myself. I had to come to terms with all the disheartening things I had said to myself and voiced out loud so that I could forgive myself. Every cut and burn? I forgive you. Every lie of protection? I forgive you. Writing those words down on paper allowed God's saving grace to work in me to heal and redeem. (See Appendix F)

4. **I had to be willing to lean in.** I surrendered to Him and laid it at the foot of the cross. I asked for the strength to forgive myself (and others). I asked God to soften my heart. He is willing; I just had to let Him do what He needed to do in my heart. This meant letting go of the control—especially the perceived control. It meant putting my trust in God when every other person broke my trust. It meant staying teachable because when we fully let go we can expect God to begin molding us into our redemption story.

Being abused as a child and raped as a young teenager deeply affects you. It wasn't a surprise that I struggled with identity issues. It wasn't a surprise that I had destructive behaviors or physical ailments. It wasn't a surprise that numbness crept into my heart the way ants march toward an unattended picnic. I hated myself for so long that the self-hatred, the continuous feelings of being inadequate, coupled with the guilt and shame of my past was causing me to bleed to death. My self-hatred bullied me into broken submission.

Our brokenness is what needs to be accepted. Accepting our imperfections is a step in healing that needs to be shouted from the rooftops.

> We cannot become whole without filling the cracks that have made us become broken.

My friend and her husband were stationed in Japan and she loved learning about the culture and different practices. She once called me excited about a practice called kintsugi (kin-su-gi). She had explained that it was an ancient Japanese art where pottery that is damaged (cracked and having large fissures or holes) are repaired using lacquer mixed with powdered gold. Her story described a clay pot that had many cracks. It was a pot that was loved and widely used. With wear and tear these cracks became visible. Larger and larger, until the water that it held would seep through the cracks. This pot could no longer serve its purpose. Through kintsugi, instead of going back to the potter to mold another one, the broken pot's cracks are filled with this golden mixture. The gold makes its way into the cracks, sealing them and forging it into something new and something stronger than the original.

As we heal from our traumas and learn to forgive ourselves, that is who we become, stronger than the original. As we let God deal with our biggest critic, as we surrender our hurts, our pains and our insecurities, He cradles us in His arms as He forges us into something new, something stronger than when we first fell at His feet. The holes of my past, the cracks from my tears are re-fired and filled with God's incredible golden mercy and love. It is through His mercy that we come to know our self-worth. He helps us to discover that we are fearfully and wonderfully made (Psalm 139:14).

> Mistakes do not negate the fact that we are worthy to be loved, wanted, cherished and adored.

chapter eight

AT ARM'S LENGTH

My family has always been very much into martial arts. My dad and uncle would teach us Kenpo as children. Kenpo is said to be a type of karate that is influenced by both Chinese and Japanese karate. It is not an offensive weapon, but one of defense to protect yourself when needed. My dad thought it was important that we learn Kenpo, like he did to successfully defend ourselves when he couldn't protect us himself.

I remember one time we were at my uncle's house doing yet another training session. We all stood in a circle and, using breathing techniques with a correctly balanced chi, we were to take a punch in our gut from my dad.

This wasn't just a "you're my kid so I'm taking it easy on you" punch. This was a "be ready or you're going to regret it" kind of punch.

I remember standing with my feet shoulder width apart. My arms were to my side at a forty-five degree angle. My fists were clenched and my eyes were closed, ready and focused to take the hit. I'd listen as my dad made his way around the circle, "Tsssss!" with a thump to a mid-section. Every kiai (k-ai-aa) meant he was getting closer to me: the end of the circle. "Tsssss!" This one came right next to me. I took a deep breath, lifted and slightly turned my right foot in hopes to brace the impact.

"Tsssss!"

At the age of approximately 10 I was hit in the gut by a grown man and I didn't flinch. I didn't lose my breath. I didn't falter. I stood my ground, with an apparent centered and controlled chi, and successfully was able to complete the exercise. I was pretty darn proud of myself thinking I had begun to learn and understand how to protect myself.

When my life took a tailspin, with the wind and the rain making it much harder to pull my life plane up I'd think about that day. The day when I, a little girl barely five feet tall, stood her ground and took a punch in the gut. I saw a girl that was strong and invincible. I saw a girl that was determined and so very strong willed. I saw a girl who could defend herself. The girl I no longer was. Realizing that, I'd go into a bigger emotional tailspin trying to figure out how I got so far off course.

My life plane had crashed when I decided to dance in the rain and be blindsided by what I thought was love. When it did, I had to learn a different way to protect myself. The only way I knew how was to build walls. I built really tall and strong walls around my heart. I thought I had to. I built walls to protect me from the hurt that was within. I built walls to protect me from the hurt that I felt hurled at me. I built my walls because it was the only thing I knew to do to survive. It provided me with a sense of protection and most of all comfort. Not having walls up meant I would be vulnerable. In fact, I never wanted to be vulnerable again. Vulnerability meant weakness, and weakness meant someone could hurt me all over again. It meant lying on the cold hard floor being kicked all over again. I wasn't going to allow any of that to happen ever again.

Most adults who were abused as children, whether physically, mentally, verbally or sexually, will tell you that their shame bound them to silence. They were terrified. They blamed themselves for what happened. They would find ways to diminish their feelings because then it wouldn't seem so real. The trauma of their past wouldn't be staring straight back at them every time they looked in a mirror. Then the betrayal wouldn't sit so heavy on their chest feeling like it was suffocating them. They would find a way to diminish every memory to protect themselves from the nightmare of what once was. And that's what I did.

After everything that had happened to me, I pushed everyone away and isolated myself. I wasn't about to tell a soul of the things that had happened. There was so much emotional pain caught up inside me, like a twister, swirling about, never quite falling back to the ground. The emotional pain was so dark that I couldn't dream of letting anyone else know about it. Why would I want them to feel what I was feeling? I was so focused on protecting my heart that I built my walls so high I needed aircraft warning lights to mark the tops of them. There was no way anyone could get in.

Building my walls meant the aircraft of my life had to find a way to stay within those walls without crashing. It also meant I had to find a way to keep other people's life planes out. So, I isolated myself from my family and friends. I isolated myself from activities I once loved doing. I spent so much time alone because it seemed safer for me and safer for everyone else. I would come up with the dumbest excuses on why I couldn't connect with my friends. I always had something to do, or always had somewhere else to be. Eventually people stopped coming around asking me to join them. For me, this seemed to be evidence that things were better when I was alone. I was able to turn those runway lights off because no one was coming into my air space.

When we deal with trauma we don't think straight. I was alone, I didn't want to be, and yet, I felt I was most authentic when I was by myself. I also felt unwanted. Through the years the most important thing was to make others proud of me, to be who others wanted me to be just so I could feel wanted. When I finally did come out about Mr. Popular, my family didn't believe me, so I felt more unwanted than ever before. In our culture family is everything. And, by that statement, I meant everything, right? I didn't expect to be cast out by my family the way I was. I hated the way I felt. I hated who I had become. And now, it seemed, so did my family. Talk about brokenness!

I hated myself so I hurt myself because I completely and utterly felt abandoned by the people who were supposed to love me. When I cut my finger with scissors in the bathroom, I would hear my family laughing in the living room. The laughs that never seemed to be around when I was. When I burned my forearm repeatedly with the tip of a paperclip, I thought of the fun my family had living in Seattle and how we weren't even a family anymore. When I sat on that park bench contemplating ending my life the pain and trauma of my past had me on my knees begging me to go through with it.

That inner voice within me was so critical of everything I did. It was as strong as a F-22 fighter jet, circling my soul and blasting its cannon through every unbroken part of me. It circled around my walls, allowing a billow of dark clouds to cover the sky so there was always only darkness and never any light. That inner voice made sure I felt isolated and alone. It made sure I felt unwanted. And, most of all, it made sure I felt unloved.

When I was reintroduced to a life with God, I knew there was something missing in my life. As I began to learn more about God, I discovered a different God than the One I had learned about growing up. Everything He said He was, was everything I was sure I didn't want. I was managing my life as best I could. Everyone thought I was a screw up, and I was, wasn't I? I mean I had the cuts, the psyche and the life to prove it. But, God. My F-22 circled around my heart and mind when I sat on the park bench that day planning to end my life. I was set, I was ready. There was nothing left for me in my life. My family was happy when I wasn't around. I had no friends. That blade would have been my escape out of my darkness. But, God had other plans.

I didn't know then that God halted my lapse in judgement. I had spent years pushing God away, or, at least keeping Him at arm's length. Growing up, He really didn't seem to be much of a father figure in my eyes. To me He was someone I had to love, because that was what I was told to do, but I didn't have a personal relationship with Him. I never really had felt His presence in my life. Not even on that day on the park bench. Yet, somehow, He stopped me from pushing that blade deeper into my wrist and ending it all.

> Then, during my darkest hour, God sent backup.

A month before the sexual assault, I had given my life to Jesus. Little did I know that single decision was going to take me on a path that pushed me through the smoke of my fighter jet to discover compassion and mercy.

chapter nine

ISOLATION

I had gotten really good at keeping everyone at arm's length. In my mind, people weren't safe. People were the ones that hurt me. Therefore, people couldn't be trusted. People were the ones who took advantage of me, abused me and threw me away. People were the ones who took more from me, never pouring back what they took. Even people I didn't know couldn't be trusted. I had always been an introvert, but at this point in my life it became extreme. I had developed a self-diagnosed agoraphobia.

The Mayo Clinic defines agoraphobia as "a type of anxiety disorder in which you fear and avoid places or situations that might cause you to panic and make you feel trapped, helpless or embarrassed."[5] My fear of something bad happening to me put me in such a stupor when in a public place. I would feel like the walls were closing in on me, suffocating me slowly, taunting me and condemning my weaknesses.

After the sexual assault I feared I would run into him at the mall, the store or at a community event. I remember always looking around before stepping out of my car, or a building, and being just seconds from a panic attack. Who was around? Where were the nearest exits? What were the landmarks that would help me remember where my car was? Who was I with? Would they protect me? Would they understand? Would they judge me? Every decision I made outside of my home functioned out of my fight, flight, or freeze response. I began feeling threatened and anxious without even knowing what the day would hold.

These panic attacks would always come when I least expected them to. The attacks always caused my body to shake, hot tears that felt like fire would flow down my cheeks. My legs would always feel as if they were filled with lead and so heavy that I couldn't lift them. It

---

5 "Agoraphobia." Mayo Clinic, www.mayoclinic.org/diseases-conditions/agoraphobia/symptoms-causes/syc-20355987, accessed on October 2021

was as if the moment I feared, the moment he'd return to hurt me because I had told the world what he had done was going to happen in the most public of ways. It didn't matter if that wasn't a reality. It didn't matter if I lived thousands of miles away. To my psyche it was the only reality.

I had to learn during these panic attacks that the only real thing I could control was my focus. Learning to control my focus helped me understand that not all people were my enemies. So, during panic attacks I focused on the person standing beside me. Through the years it has mostly been my husband. He's gotten so good at knowing the signs that he immediately stops what we are doing and helps me focus on my breathing (breathing exercises are always a great coping technique). Once I learned to control my hyperventilating I could focus on the present. I could focus on my husband's features. I could focus on the calming of his voice, the kindness in his green eyes or the soothing rhythm of his heartbeat. These panic attacks could last for several minutes, the after effects even longer, but focusing on what I could control always led me out of it.

The attacks had become so exhausting. I realized, though not quick enough, before I could fully understand why the enemy wanted to keep me isolated, I would need to first conquer my attacks. It took me years to conquer them. It wasn't until May of 2020, when I sat in an Airbnb kitchen with four of the strongest, kindest, loving women I know, that I was able to find breakthrough. The anxiety and panic attacks had escalated to the point that they were almost debilitating. I was grieving the loss of a foster son, and my foster dad, and I felt I was drowning.

As exhausting as these attacks were, I had learned to live with them. Accepting them as part of life. This also meant I never really asked God to take them from me. That day in May of 2020 in that kitchen was different. I felt more than just exhaustion. I felt beaten, battled, trampled. I felt I had already been drug through the mud in every which way possible. My heart was broken, my body was aching.

> Something had to give,
> or I'd never find my way back out.

You see, for nearly thirty years the devil had used my pain, my trauma to isolate me. This is one of his favorite neutralization tactics. The enemy means business and his plan for us is to kill, steal and destroy who we are. He wants to create in us a spirit of fear, of unworthiness and of discouragement. He wants to render us completely and utterly fruitless and powerless in the Kingdom of Heaven. He weaponizes every doubt we've ever had and spins it with just enough truth for us to believe it, in hopes it will debilitate us and isolate us from God and His Word. He weaponizes every insecurity we've ever had and turns it into grenades, in hopes that we will isolate ourselves from the very community that God created to help us.

The enemy loves isolation and isolation takes many forms. In my case, isolation looked like self-reliance, busyness, distractions and shame. When he can isolate us from like-minded, Spirit-filled people he can gain a foothold in our thoughts. On my journey to find my identity, the most damage the enemy did was when I chose to isolate myself. Isolation allows the enemy to whisper louder and louder the half-truths. I had listened to those half-truths so often I had embraced them as my identity.

In order for me to find my true identity I had to come face to face with my desire for isolation. To do that I first had to come to the realization that **Jesus wants to give me life**. The life Jesus gives us is a life without shame. A life without hiding. A life where I wouldn't have to struggle to catch my breath as I dealt with another anxiety attack. A life that gave me everything in abundance (John 10:10) from joy, to strength, to the deepest desires of my heart.

Second, I had to acknowledge **the devil wants to destroy me**. As odd as it may sound, it brought me comfort, because it meant, the enemy was trying what he could to destroy and silence my story. He was finding a way to distract me and to prohibit me from accepting Whose I was.

> The greater our story, the greater God's plan.

The enemy didn't want my story to be heard.

And lastly, dealing with my need for isolation meant I had to come to grips with the fact that **Jesus created us to be a part of a community**. Isolating myself kept God from having the opportunity to work inside of me through others. When I laid my agoraphobia at the foot of Jesus that morning I wasn't afraid to stand up and walk away from it. I knew between the grace and mercy from God and the support of these women I no longer needed to bear the burden of my anxiety any longer.

The morning those ladies prayed for me was the last time I have had an anxiety or panic attack. After twenty plus years God healed me from anxiousness. I could finally take a deep breath, letting it fill my lungs with joy. Losing those attacks from my life was another great hurdle. Since that morning I have found a freedom that feels so incredibly surreal. We cannot find our identity in Christ without complete freedom.

When I built my walls around my heart, I intended to keep everything bad away from me. What I didn't realize was that isolating myself, building those walls as high as I could also ensured that all the good never came in as well. I had to allow God to work within my heart to understand that there are bad people in the world, but there will also be people He sends my way that are safe. People who want to pour life, love and laughter into me. People who stand firm in their beliefs in Jesus and help me stand when I don't have the strength to stand. People who will settle in beside me when the waters of my storm crash over the sides of my boat. People who would become my community. When I found my community, when I stopped willingly isolating myself, it was then that I found hope. It was then that I was willing to figure out this identity thing.

chapter ten

KINDRED SPIRITS

Shortly after my dad's passing in 2014, I became really good friends with a girl in my office. I spent half of 2014 losing three of the most important people in my life. All my friends were in Hawaii while I was crumbling in Oregon. When my husband and I flew back to Hawaii to attend his grandfather's memorial she was our last minute dog/house sitter.

My dogs mean the world to me. I will protect them like I would protect any of my children. When we returned home from our week of travels, they were alive, in one piece and loved her. This spoke volumes to me. If my dogs could trust her, then so could I. This was an unlikely friendship, but a friendship nonetheless. It was a friendship born out of great need. It was built during a time of grief when I needed a friend.

We became best friends. One day we were hanging out and I felt the need to tell her all the things wrong with me that I thought would make her walk away from our friendship. Every shame I could think of I told her. Every guilt, I told her. Every fault, failure and misstep, I told her. Every quirk and weakness, I told her. I wanted her to begin to see that everyone left me in my life for a reason. The sooner she understood that, the sooner she'd realize there were great reasons for her to leave me too. I tried to have her walk away because I didn't want to have to go through the pain and loss of being left again.

"I'm not going anywhere."

The last time four words changed my world it wasn't a good thing. This time, a new set of four words opened the door to the realization that not all people are bad and not all people are untrustworthy.

I could name on one hand all the people who actually made me feel safe. I was in desperate need to find someone that I could talk to. Someone who would listen. I had spent nearly all of my life keeping people and God at arm's length. There was so much pain from the losses I had suffered that year that I didn't care that my heart would be vulnerable. And, God knew. He saw the grief dismantling me and sent someone who understood isolation to come alongside me, to help me understand people were safe.

> God created us to be in relationship with Him and with people.

I didn't understand that. So, it's no wonder I didn't think it necessary for me to be part of something. I didn't want people close. Instead of being part of a community, I was adamant in masquerading through life with masks that showed I had it all together, I was strong or that I didn't need help from others. Individualism was so important to me. I had survived my life standing on my own two feet. The trauma in my life ingrained in me that being alone, and never asking for help, was okay. In fact, it was more than okay, it was ideal. Why would I depend on people if I didn't need them? Why would I depend on people if I didn't trust them? Why would I depend on people if they always hurt me? If my masks illuminated that I was a fighter, why did I need to do anything differently?

Once I realized people were safe, God continued to draw me into community life. God once again met a prodigal's need, like He has done so many times before. It didn't hit me until I sat in that Airbnb kitchen. God had revitalized my spirit by intentionally placing in my path storm chasing women who could help me extinguish the tornado that was wreaking havoc in my life. A community of people that love others like God loves them. A community of people who bless and encourage, who support and build up. He had brought me into a community of kindred spirits who read and lived out the Gospel in their daily lives.

What I've noticed, is when we've gone through trauma, hurt and pain, God purposefully engulfs us in love and mercy. For me, His love and mercy kept surrounding me with people who loved me through my healing. That is what community is all about. It's people who make us feel comfortable in our own skin. People who love us despite our faults and failures. People who encourage and pour into our lives. If there is anything I have learned the last three years, it is that I am stronger, healthier, and happier as I grow into the woman God has always intended me to be.

As I continue to grow, I think of the people who God has placed in my life. They are all so very important to me. They all play certain roles in my life, each supporting me, loving me, praying with and for me. All of these people have the same characteristics in common:

They love like Jesus. This world doesn't need any more negativity. When I look for people who I will open my heart to, I want someone who chooses love. Jesus sat with harlots and murderers. He didn't bother sitting with priests or those who were superficially religious. John 15:12 (NIV) says, "My command is this: Love each other as I have loved you." The people I surround myself with love like Jesus loves.

They understand and accept the real me. I have a lot of faults. I've made a lot of mistakes. Having people who look past my faults and failures to love me have helped me to approach God in my own humility. Having people who knew and accepted that my faith was weak (Romans 14:1), and didn't use that to make me stumble, taught me to love and accept the real me, just like they have.

They call me out on my nonsense. A real friend speaks the truth even when it hurts.

> Find someone who can lovingly call you out on your hogwash thinking.

Theses friends can find fault in the behavior and still love us, the person. Ephesians 4:15 says that speaking the truth in love will allow us to grow and exhibit the character of Christ. Even if I drive them crazy with my emotions and nonsense, they still love me through it.

They build me up. In every single way possible—spiritually, physically, mentally and emotionally—we all need people who make us better. We need people who encourage us to be better. People who push us to reach our wildest dreams. "As iron sharpens iron, so one person sharpens another." (Proverbs 27:17 NIV). Finding a community that loves us, lets us cry on their shoulder, and then takes our hand to keep going, has been an invaluable source of growth for me. Them not allowing me to give up is the reason I am here today.

They pray for me. I knew God blessed me with a community when I confessed my deepest regret, and they went to God for me. They met me where I was and closed the gap between me and God. And when I wasn't in a dark pit or suffering, they still remembered me in their prayers, just as Paul did for Rome (Romans 1:9-10).

In the last two years I have found myself around people that I've thrived with. My mind is clearer. My heart is kinder. My attitude is more positive. With these people I want to love like Jesus, pray and praise like Hannah and have the faith of Abraham. Surrounding myself with like-minded people who have squashed my insecurities and fear of being alone, has been a catalyst for deeper healing.

As I sat across from the four women who had just prayed for me, I realized they were my people. They were the people that saw and heard the highs and lows of my life. They were the people who laughed so hard with me they cried, and the ones who cried with me during my deepest heartaches. They were my community. My tribe.

I have others outside of these women who are a part of my community as well. Like my therapist. She may not be a best friend, or go to my church, but she fits those characteristics. She isn't afraid to be real with me and call me on my foolishness. She prays for me and speaks healing spiritually, emotionally and mentally in my life.

Or the women scattered across the U.S. that I met on my writing retreat. They, too, love Jesus. They aren't afraid to pray for and with me. We challenge each other to be the very best we can be. In the short time I have known them we have celebrated small and big successes together and cried for the good and the bad. Most of all, we have poured life into each other's hearts.

While these three groups of people have helped me anchor my ship, I've been on a mission to connect even more. I am part of multiple support groups covering topics such as fostering, infertility and faith. I also build my network by attending conferences, retreats, various trainings and book clubs. Finding these connections has allowed me to not stay stagnant on my journey to unleashing my true identity. It was important for me to keep connecting with people who I could learn from, grow with, pray for and pray with. I'm building my community with different walks of life because I had come to understand my community shouldn't be consisting of a single crewman. So, I've invited others in. There is more than enough room on the ship for chief hands, stewards, deck cadets and seamen for there is no growth when there is no learning.

part three

FINDING RESTORATION

chapter eleven

SHELTERED SAFE

Do you remember the first place you ever felt safe?

When I lived in Seattle, my family had a newspaper delivery route. I think we actually had four routes. When it was time to deliver the paper, we did it as a family. It was sort of our own family business. I remember the adventures we had driving from house to house, jumping out of the back of the station wagon to deliver each paper. Adventures included when my oldest sister was bit by an ankle biter, my other sister jumped out of her skin when she came face to face with a Komodo dragon and the house with the long driveway where we believed the statue of an ordinary man standing guard at the front of the house was, in fact, once a real man who passed on and the family couldn't let him go so they stuffed him. For a five-year-old these were grand adventures.

My favorite newspaper route adventure happened on a Sunday. Each Sunday we would wrap the gargantuan papers in thicker rubber bands, and sometimes in plastic depending on the weather, at three o'clock in the morning. We would get our route done then we would head directly to church. We attended a little white chapel church. At five years old I was already an introvert. I always wanted to stay with my mom and dad while my siblings went to the basement for Sunday school. It was there, while listening to hymns being sung out of the old hymnals, that I first came face to face with Jesus.

Every Sunday morning, on the floor under the pew my parents were sitting in, as the congregation sang, I cuddled in a ball enveloped in God's love and fell asleep. You'll say, "For a five-year-old having to wake up before three o'clock in the morning, falling asleep would come as no surprise." This wasn't a dead tired kind of sleep. This wasn't an "I'm bored" kind of sleep. This wasn't even a tantrum-spent-energy kind of sleep. I can remember humming the songs as my dad's foot tapped beside me. I remember feeling content, safe, protected.

I can remember feeling the arms of Jesus wrapping around me rocking me softly to sleep.

I have spent years comparing my walk with Christ to those Sundays. As the years have gone by, and I have learned more and more about who Jesus is and what He stands for, I've come to the realization that it's true: even if I didn't know it then, God has always been saying, "Pearl, Pearl, here I am."

While healing from our trauma begins with our journey through self-discovery and understanding who we really are, knowing God's voice is critical on that path. Not knowing the voice of God prohibits us from claiming the blessings on our lives and becoming who God always intended us to be. If we cannot hear the voice of God, those heavily guarded walls we have built around our hearts will never break. So, what can we do to ensure we can hear the voice of God?

First, stop the noise. Do you know what muffles the voice of Jesus when He speaks to you? What stops you from hearing that still small voice? What is it that blocks you from hearing Jesus?

For me there are a handful of things. Human pain really gets me. I can feel someone else's pain so acutely as if it were my own. If they hurt, I hurt. Pleasing people can prevent me from hearing His voice. I still find myself trying to be someone I am not in hopes that I either am liked by others or I am trying to make someone else's life easier for them (even if it makes it harder on me). Rejection can silence the still small voice of Jesus. Rejection was present every time a bad thing happened to me. I knew the feeling of rejection was there. "Do you see me? Do you love me? Will you leave me?" When I feel rejected things get muted. Busyness keeps me from hearing too. Being so busy that I'm overwhelmed, trying to be in too many places at once will exhaust me and burn me out. Trying to be a super mom, an incredible wife and an invaluable employee, without hearing the word of God, can keep me from hearing the voice that brings peace.

My brain has so much noise.

Removing the noise allows me to hear God whispering in my ear. Revelations 3:20 (NASB) says "Behold, I stand at the door and knock; if anyone hears My voice and opens the door, I will come in to him and will dine with him, and he with Me." Jesus wants us to draw near to Him and He will draw near to us (James 4:8).

> We don't have to hear Jesus from an amplified speaker. We just need to hear Him from a tin-can telephone.

We just need to welcome Him in and be willing to receive the intimate love of our Father.

I grew up knowing God on a surface level. That meant I was trained to know where in the Bible a particular book could be found. I was trained to know the "main" stories like the creation story, Noah's Ark, Moses and the commandments, the birth of Jesus and the Resurrection. I was trained to memorize verses like John 3:16, Proverbs 3:5-6 and Matthew 5:3-10 and 6:9-13. But I never really knew or understood who Jesus was. It was never personal. To me there was no humanity in Jesus. It was always about religion. It wasn't about matters of the heart. It was strictly, "Obey or you're a heathen."

> My Pastor once said that God will overlook our doctrine and answer to our faith.

When I was growing up, religion was everything to my family. When I say religion, I mean we devoted ourselves to public worship. The spitting image of what everyone thought Christians should be. We were acutely aware of how we presented ourselves in church, all the things we said and did, because anything negative affected our standings in the church. It wasn't simply about pleasing

God and loving Him faithfully. It was all about crossing all our t's and dotting all our i's to appear *holy*. That was our primary goal, to be *holy*. I didn't want to be *holy*. That felt fake and forced. I wanted to serve a God who loved me and didn't keep score on the millions of times I stumbled. That is when I found intimacy.

Intimacy is personal. Intimacy is a matter of the heart. Intimacy with Jesus doesn't force us to sign on the dotted line or be at a certain point in our Christian walk to have a relationship with Him. We only need to confess our sins and come as we are. It is about fellowshipping with Him. Having an intimate and personal relationship with Jesus is about knowing the Father, knowing who He is, what He does, and what He calls us to be. Intimacy is being called the one Jesus dearly loves, as John was called (John 13:23), and being able to lay our head on Jesus' chest and hear His heart. There is nothing more personal than knowing, truly knowing, our identity in Christ. Being intimate with Jesus is a step toward solving our identity crisis.

The thing with being in an intimate and personal relationship with God, is that in order to know our identity, not only will there be restoration from trauma, but there is also a lot of breaking and forging. As we step forward to find our identity in Him, we will be sifted. We will be shaken and tempted to give up, to let go. We will be tested. We need to know what God's identity is in order for us to know who we are in Him. He will allow us to be transformed from sand to gemstones into the most exquisite pearl. Hold steady, listen to Him call. He will not leave us in the middle of the refining process. He wants to take hold of your hand and walk with you. Listen. Do you hear Him calling out to you? Hear Him as He says, "Beloved! Beloved! Here I am." Hear His words today. Be encouraged, strengthened by His love. Be engulfed, sheltered safe, in His compassion and mercy. When you are ready, stand up and walk.

chapter twelve

A WALK WITH GOD

What would it feel like to take a walk with Jesus?

I am a dreamer. I have always been a dreamer. My imagination has always taken me to far-away lands, lands where there was love and peace and no pain. It isn't surprising then to know that my favorite coping skill is The Happy Place (see Chapter 2 "Here I Am", page 19).

I remember a time when I attended a Women's Conference and we did a *soaking prayer*. I had done a couple of different soaking prayers before, but this one was a little different. For those unfamiliar with soaking prayers, it's time set aside to "soak", be still, lean in and rest in the presence of the Lord. I've had soaking prayers with light instrumentals playing in the background. I've had soaking prayers with complete stillness. I've done it with groups and alone. It's about building intimacy with God. For me, soaking prayers are about leaning into what Holy Spirit is specifically saying to me.

This particular soaking prayer was more of a soaking prompt. Using imagery, the exercise took me to my happy place by engaging my senses. The prompting asked questions like, what did I see? What did I feel? What do I hear? The prompts led me to an encounter with Jesus. This experience brought me to my knees. It wasn't my imagination trying to pretend a different reality. This experience was real. God profoundly spoke to me that day. The experience completely changed my life and the trajectory that it was on.

As I rested in the presence of the Lord during this soaking prayer, I was instantly brought to my happy place. I stood on a beach I had visited so many times in my childhood. The sand was soft and warm under my feet. The ocean was an incredible warm blue, its waves crashing gently upon the shore. The rhythmic sound sent music to my ears as it beat against the shoreline. I looked around and I saw palm trees further up shore. Under one of the palm trees I saw my dad's mom, my Mama, sitting with her big Filipino sun hat with the sweetest smile on her face. She was content, watching the pattern of the waves hit the shore. I saw my dad standing knee deep in the water, watching his line bob up and down. He was the happiest I have ever seen him earth-side. When I saw my Dad and his mom, I knew God wanted my heart calmed and opened. I heard the waves being serenaded by the sound of children laughing, as they ran in and out along the shoreline. I felt the sun gently warming my face and shoulders.

As I turned, I saw Jesus coming toward me. My heart filled with both joy and sadness. On His head I could see the crown of thorns. My heart sank knowing that crown was placed on His head to purchase my freedom. Blood slowly trickled down His face, but He didn't cry out in agony.

> **Instead all I saw in His eyes was love.
> Love for me.**

There was such deep compassion and mercy in His eyes. He stopped in front of me, clothed in white, barefoot in the sand. He reached out to me. I looked at His palms and saw the scars from the nails that pinned Him to the cross.

I fell to my knees weeping. I heard my heart cry out, "Lord, what have I done!? You put Your life on that cross that I may have life. My heart is filled with immense gratitude and sorrow. To see what You had to bear to give me life is gutting me. I am so unworthy to be called Your daughter."

Jesus took my hands and gently pulled me to my feet. He lifted my head as tears streamed down my face. The love and tenderness in His eyes makes me feel so unworthy. He smiles and calls me by name, "Pearl, sweet girl, look at Me." I struggle to lift my eyes up. How could I look up? I was so embarrassed by all of my shortcomings. He cupped my face between his nail scarred hands and gently lifted it up so my eyes meet His. As soon as I looked into His eyes my body, mind and soul were encompassed with comfort and peace. He rubbed His thumbs across my cheeks to wipe my tears, "My child, you may not see it now. But there will come a day when you will realize just how much I love you. Just how much you mean to Me. There will come a day when you find yourself worthy of your crown and realize Whose you are."

That year I had spent so much time on my knees, being sifted. God had been working on me to release the burdens I had been carrying. The plans I had in place for myself, God had been reworking to fit His own. Every part of my life felt as if He was clearing out everything that didn't align to His purpose. He had emphasized healing in my life that year, requiring me to face the trauma of my past and the anger that I didn't even know was there. All the while feeling absolutely crushed.

When I attended this women's conference, I felt trampled. I felt beaten. I felt bone weary. I expected to receive something from God, but I didn't expect *that*. Though it was what I absolutely needed, I didn't expect Jesus to wipe my tears and tell me how much He loved me. I didn't expect Him to say I meant anything to Him. I didn't expect Him to declare I belonged to Him. What I didn't know that day was He was preparing a shift in my relationship with Him. He was preparing a shift in my relationship with others. He was preparing a shift for a season where the only way through was leaning on Him.

Two days after that conference I got sick. Eight days after the conference I found myself in the back of an ambulance in the wee hours of the morning afraid for my life. I was admitted to the hospital where I was isolated from my world, my community and my family for an entire week. I had spent the entire year learning to be the woman God intended me to be. As I lay in that hospital bed, it suddenly felt like my entire world was upended. God intended for me to claim the identity He had given me, but I could barely breathe to save my life much less exert any energy to fight for that identity. I suddenly found myself imprisoned by my old self and its old thinking. A sickness that shackled me to my bed also shackled my thoughts. I struggled with doubt and anxiousness as if I never had won victory over them. I was held captive by the taunting by the enemy that I would never wear that crown.

I knew that God would meet me by faith despite the mental torture brought on by the sickness. I knew even just a little bit of faith could break the chains no matter how dark the dungeon seemed.

> With the small amount of faith God would meet me where I was.

So, I did what I could with the microbic amount of energy I had.

I cried a lot. God had wiped my tears away before and I knew He'd do it again. I felt helpless. The first three weeks after my return home from the hospital, I could barely lift my head up on my own. My husband had to walk me to the bathroom that was fifteen feet from my bed. It took me a while to eat a single meal on my own. I cried but I leaned on God knowing this would pass.

I journaled a lot. More like doodled my feelings. Drawing was easier for me at that point than writing, so I doodled my prayers. It would not make sense to anyone who opened up my prayer journal, but God knew. And that was all I needed to keep going.

I asked for help a lot. It is incredibly humbling to be unable to pick up your cup and having to ask your three-year-old for help. I asked for prayers from my tribe. I swallowed my pride and allowed our community to bring us dinners and snacks to love on us. I asked for laughter from my children. I asked for strength from and for my husband.

I read a lot. I had written down what God said to me during my soaking prayer the night I encountered Him. I reread that over and over, each time reclaiming those words for my life. I was loved. I meant something to Him. Even if I wasn't quite able to believe it, I told myself I was His. I read books like *Still* from Jenny Donnelly and *Empty Arms* from Pam Vredevelt to continue learning and refining myself.

But, mostly, I soaked a lot. I soaked in the presence of God, trying to feel even just a tiny bit of how I was feeling before getting sick. I soaked in the present moments with my family. So often in my life I had been on the go, trying to do this, trying to accomplish that. The down time allowed me important personal time with them. I soaked in worship music. Music that could help my soul feel uplifted.

During the most physical challenge of my life, I allowed God to walk with me, to teach me and to mold me. I walked with God, allowing Him to carry every burden I had. I walked with Him and learned my strength came from Him. Understanding who I was meant that I had to trust God in every aspect of my life. I had to rely on His promises, even when the jail cell didn't offer much hope or light.

> I had to confront and surrender to the fact that when I walked with God, He was actually carrying me.

chapter thirteen

CLAIMING MY INHERITANCE

How would it feel to be known as His Beloved?

On the opening night of a writing retreat for this book, I walked into the chapel and there sat four wooden crosses. Knowing on Calvary there were only three crosses, I thought it odd but I was mesmerized and drawn to them. As I waited for others to gather in the chapel, I stared at these crosses. I have always understood the magnitude of Jesus dying on the cross, but something about those four stood out to me. Was it the fourth cross that made me yearn for answers? What kind of symbolism did it stand for? Or, was it the red paint dripping on the cross bars representing the sins of the world with every drop? As the crosses were explained I felt a stirring.

I had been battling my self-hatred for as long as I could remember. If I did something good, my subconscious would belittle me, saying I could have done it better. If I won something, my brain would laugh and tell me I got lucky. It was a constant battle regarding my value. When God told me to write about finding my identity a battle raged within me. I wasn't sure I knew what my identity was. How could I write about identity if I didn't know my own? How could someone like me, who still questioned her worth, tell someone else they needed to stop questioning theirs?

The first night of that writing retreat, as I walked toward the cross, I touched shoulders with an incredible woman of God. I had been to a handful of her events but never had a conversation with her. She didn't really know who I was, but what she said changed something inside of me, "I see the Lord telling you that you are His pearl of great price. That you have been through much refining. Just like a pearl goes through its cultivation process, so have you.

> Jesus sees you as a hidden treasure.

As His daughter who He sold everything for. He has sharpened you for such a time as this. Let Him love you through it."

As she whispered these words to me streams of tears poured down my face. Steadying myself, I walked to the cross. Putting my hands on the wet paint picturing the blood he shed for my sins I wept. I wept for every ounce of shame that I carried, heavy on my shoulders. I wept for every fear of not being enough, for not being loved. I wept for every wrong done to me, and every wrong I had done to someone else. As I stood at that cross, my body shook with the years of disgrace I had carried on my shoulders. Touching the cross bar, picturing Jesus' arms outstretched across it, a wave of emotions swept over me. This was what it meant to be loved by Him. Intense feelings of gratitude poured through me. With my hands on the cross, in awe and wonder I finally realized just how much I meant to Him.

The last two years God had been working on my heart. For two years He had sent people my way trying to build me up, to encourage me, and to help me see myself as God sees me. For two years He had poured gold into my broken vessel, that I might finally see myself as something other than a screw up, someone who was alone, unloved, unworthy and broken. That night at the cross, laying my hands on His feet, He whispered to me to let go of the pain that I had let define me. He whispered to let go of the betrayal that I had kept hidden away. He whispered to let go of the unworthiness that had stifled my growth.

> God hunched over me, cradling me as I wept for every heartbreak that has ever happened in my life.

He held me closer as tear after tear ran down my face. I heard Him whisper, "Beloved, it's okay," as my whole body shook, letting it all go.

There is something about the cross, that when we go to it completely bare, completely vulnerable and completely open to God touching our heart, it changes, transforms and renews us. We feel things differently. We see things differently. We think things differently. On my knees, my head in my hands, crying out to Jesus, every pain, every trauma, every fear dissipated. That's when I heard Him say, "Daughter, there you are." Suddenly, the scales were lifted from my eyes and I knew Whose I was.

Why, on this journey of healing and reformation, was it so important that I knew Whose I was?

That night at the retreat I walked in feeling completely alone. I was completely out of my comfort zone. I had no one to hide behind. I had no one to start the conversation for me. I had no one to fall back on when the energy of where I was got too much. I stood on the ledge and I alone had to be willing to take the plunge. I alone had the choice to stay where I was, always doubting, always anxious, always hurting, or choose to lean into God, believe I was there for a purpose and claim my inheritance.

I had spent so many years worrying about everyone else's opinions of me. I had allowed those opinions to shape my opinions of myself. It affected every aspect of my life. It took hold of every emotion, every relationship, every path I took. When my low opinions of myself had a stronghold in my life, I forgot, or likely ignored, how God saw me. I forgot what He felt for me was never changing. How He saw me was never changing. In a world full of darkness and hate, He alone had abundant love for me. Me! The same girl who had burned herself. The same girl who had put herself down. The same girl who pushed everyone, especially Him, away. Me, the same girl who felt she was unlovable.

He died on the cross thinking of you and me. He died on the cross so that we could experience fullness of joy, grace, mercy and compassion. He died on the cross that we may receive emotional healing, physical healing and spiritual healing. He died on the cross for our redemption. That is our inheritance. Our inheritance is in Him. In order for me to claim my inheritance I had to accept that I was His heir. I had to accept that I am all that He says I am.

Who, exactly, does God say we are? In order for me to answer that question for myself, I had to stop dictating my own value. I had to stop playing mind games with myself. I had to take a step back, stop controlling the narrative and accept what I was hearing God call me:

His Daughter. 2 Corinthians 6:18 (TPT) the Lord declares, "I will be a true Father to you, and you will be my beloved sons and daughters." As a prodigal child, I had walked away from my God given title. But, then, He reminds me of the stillness and calm of the mornings when He'd rock me to sleep under those church pews all those years ago.

Beloved. To be greatly loved. He so greatly loves us that He gave His only Son to die on the cross so that we would not have to (John 3:16). He so greatly loves us that He rejoices over us with gladness and singing (Zephaniah 3:17). He so greatly loves us that He lavishes His love on us and calls us His beloved (1 John 3:1).

A Warrior. A warrior isn't always someone who is in the middle of battle, fighting for glory. A warrior is someone who, by faith, with three stones killed a giant.

A warrior is someone who, by faith, takes a stand against his people knowing they'd go against him. We can do all things through Christ who strengthens us (Philippians 4:13) for He equips us for every battle.

Forgiven. Someone once told me *we can't be paralyzed by our past in our present response to Jesus.* I had to understand that my past does not define me. Who I was then, is not who I am now. I am daring to live as a forgiven woman. I found not accepting the forgiveness He has given me only hardened my heart. He has forgiven everything I have done because He is a lover that does not keep score (1 Corinthians 13:5).

A Conqueror. We are more than conquerors through Him who loves us (Romans 8:37). Through God's grace I have overcome trauma. I have defeated depression and anxiety. I have withstood hardship. A conqueror will crush everything that is thrown their way as they lean on Jesus. Putting my faith in Jesus is the only reason I have been able to win the battle of self-hatred, depression and fear.

Restored. When something is restored it always looks, feels, and sounds better than at the start of restoration. God has taken my most broken pieces and has put me back together stronger and more resilient. God said that

He restores my health and heals my wounds (Jeremiah 30:17) and He has.

Most of all, I am **His.** He chose me. He didn't look around, shrugging His shoulders, thinking He guesses I'm okay for the job. He didn't choose me by accident. Before He laid eyes on me, He called out my name. Jeremiah 1:5 (NIV) says "Before I formed you in the womb I knew you, before you were born I set you apart." He had chosen me long before I had chosen Him.

I had to come to a place in my life where nothing was blocking me from going to God. I had to step out without my husband, without my best friends, without the comforts of someone else and be honest with God. He already knows every heartache I have ever had, and the heartaches to come, but I had to be willing to say, "Lord, this is where it hurt." I had to hear Him call me by name, tell me I'm forgiven, call me restored and not argue saying, "But, God..."

I had to come to understand that my "But, God" excuses were a defensive mechanism. They were the last wall around my heart that needed to be torn down. For years I struggled to understand how, in the places that I couldn't love and accept myself, God would love and accept me. To be able to accept all God says you are, you have to go to Him bare. I was so focused on protecting my heart under my own strength that I was missing the point. It should never have been a defense mechanism. Instead, what it should have been, was a declaration of His goodness:

But, God is the God that redeems.

But, God is the God that brings joy in the mourning.

But, God is the God that gives grace abundantly.

But, God is the God that strengthens, comforts and heals.

Bowing before Him at the cross and declaring all that He was, I realized that if I could just take hold of my inheritance, if I could see myself as all that God says I am, He could restore all that was broken within me. If I could stand as His daughter, He would give me unspeakable joy that would overshadow all of my life's pain and sorrow. If I could take the name of Beloved, He would restore my life.

> We can't be paralyzed by our past in our present response to Jesus.

chapter fourteen

GOD OF RESTORATION

What would it feel like to have all my brokenness restored?

An old friend from high school found me on Facebook a few weeks back. She and I weren't close. She was more of a flower child. Me? Not so much. In the course of a few hours we chatted about everything. Nothing was really off limits. We talked about our families and our careers. We talked about how things have been going since the world shutdown in early 2020. We talked as if we actually knew each other.

"I was drawn to your kids." She told me. "I searched for you. I don't know why. I was looking at old yearbooks, saw a candid picture of us in some class we were in together and thought to find you on Facebook." She wasn't sure it was me, because my profile picture is of my kids. My banner is a picture of the ocean. She reached out anyway.

Honestly, I didn't even know we had ever been in the same class. I had to dig deep to remember who she was. So much of my life back then I had forgotten in order to protect myself. I had burned or ripped apart all of the old year books I had. The only thing I had left from that school was my varsity letter. I stayed away from our class ten-year reunion. I had already declined our twentieth. I didn't understand why she'd seek me out.

"I knew you got married and I knew your last name," she continued. "I know, not creepy at all. Beauty of a small town, right?"

I laughed a little trying to not feel uncomfortable. She was right, it was kinda creepy. We had already been talking back and forth for about thirty minutes. She didn't seem like some girl that was looking to figure out where I was and get back at me for all the horrible things I did in high school. "We definitely come from a small town," I quipped back.

By this time, I had already looked her profile up trying to put the pieces together. I pictured her smiling, trying to relax, knowing I wasn't going to call her out for her creepy, stalker-ish hunt for me. "I can't explain it. You'll think I'm weird, if you don't already. But I felt something tugging at my heart the moment I saw that picture. When I searched for you online something about your profile picture called out to me. I had to message you to see if it was you."

Another half hour passed before she explained that she was contemplating giving up. She didn't know what that meant, only that she was tired. She was hurting. She had walked away from her marriage. She had walked away from her family. She had walked away from God. She was looking for the final push off the cliff when she stumbled across the picture of us in high school.

I never believed that God could ever use me to bring glory to His Kingdom. I thought I had nothing to offer Him. Then I remembered God doesn't necessarily look for the wealthy, put together sort of people to advance the Kingdom. He uses people like Rahab to help bring down the walls of Jericho (Joshua 2), a Samaritan woman to be His witness (John 4:1-26), Jael who drove a peg into the skull of God's enemies (Judges 4:17-22). He uses people like Paul as a catalyst to build the early church (Acts 9:1-31) and King David who was called a man after God's own heart (1 Samuel 13:14). If He could use them, He could use me.

That's the miraculous thing about restoration. Restoration in people's lives is a huge thing to God. You cannot tell me a single story of someone so broken that God couldn't step in and do something. Restoration is what the enemy wants to prevent. Restoration in us means glory to God. Restoration in us means sharing the gospel. Restoration in us means the enemy has lost once again. It is a promise from God that there is a better life for us.

Trauma put darkness in my heart. Who I was in high school is not the same girl I am today. And that is the most powerful thing about restoration. It freed me from a life that was filled with shame and guilt.

> Restoration freed me from a life of secrecy and isolation.

In 1 Peter 5:10 (TPT) it says, "And then, after your brief suffering, the God of all loving grace, who has called you to share in his eternal glory in Christ, will personally and powerfully restore you and make you stronger than ever. Yes, he will set you firmly in place and build you up."

And He has.

From the moment I said yes as a teenager during a family camp service, and all the yeses in between, He has built me up. He has restored the little girl curled up in a ball on the concrete floor. He has given strength to the young girl who froze during an assault. He has restored the balance that depression and anxiety stole from me. He has built up a faith through healing and deliverance that was once fragile. He has restored the identity of a prodigal child, rejoicing in my return because I was once lost and now am found.

As my friend cried through the conversation, she shared how she felt abandoned by everyone she has known. How she's felt alone for so long. She couldn't understand how people who claimed to love her could make her feel so isolated, so unworthy, so unloved. She had begged those in her life for help, for her and for them, and no one was willing to do anything, to change anything. She kept apologizing for her breakdown and the fact that after nearly twenty years of never talking, our first conversation was this. And that's when I knew why she was reaching out to me.

You see, you can't take someone through something you have never gone through yourself. I knew intimately what she was feeling. I understood every tear that slid down her face. She was in such anguish she could not see the entire summary of her story. She only saw a cliff to jump off of, and not the ladder below her. When we take our eyes off of Jesus, we lose sight of that ladder. We lose sight of the step that He lays in front of us, by trying to read the entire chapter before the next sentence. Engulfed in her grief, her tears had created mud around her that made her feel like she was sinking.

I knew I had to share God's faithfulness in my life, so she could see there was a ladder beneath her. I shared my testimony with her. Shared the heartache of being unwanted and unseen. Shared the fear and anxiety caused by depression. Shared the loneliness and doubt that comes with feeling unloved. I told her of the darkness that threatened my very life. I shared how I often found myself in stormy waters, with barely a life buoy to keep me afloat. I explained that the thunder and lightning would disorient me, while the water would cause me to stumble in my breathing. I confessed that the more my lungs burned with each gulp of the seawater, the closer I had gotten to jumping.

As I shared God's faithfulness in my life she asked, "How could you see the lighthouse when your head was barely above the water?"

Taking a deep breath, I answered, "By having the faith of Peter to walk on water."

All the steps on coping and getting over grief weren't the foundation I needed to find healing from my trauma. They weren't the reason I claimed my inheritance. They helped, but it was Jesus. It was always Jesus. His beacon of light always shone clearly through the darkness, calling me to safety, calling me to come home. Through the raging seas and the rocky cliffs, He stood with His hands outstretched toward me. Every single time my ship turned away from Him, He kept choosing me. Every time I blared my horn to stave Him from getting close, He waited for me. Every time my boat was rocked and ready to go under, He pulled me out in the nick of time.

I explained to her that no matter what happened in my life, no matter how bad things got, even when I turned my back on God, He provided. He provided comfort. He provided healing. He provided finances. He provided health. He provided. When I was adamant that no one could ever love me, God kept telling me, "Let Me prove you wrong." And He did, time and time again.

You see, God never said this path would be easy. If it was, it wouldn't be a narrow path. But He did promise that on this path, as we rest in Him, He'd renew our strength. We would not grow tired. We would not faint. Instead, He would allow us to soar. God was willing to restore my brokenness. God wants to restore hers. And He wants to restore yours as well.

As I sit back thinking about all that I had to go through to get to where I am today, the one thing I wish I did sooner was let people in. Not denying my trauma was important. Healing from the internal pain, the scars of fear, doubt and depression was needed. But I couldn't do that without letting people in. I couldn't be restored without someone taking a hold of my hand and bridging the gap between me and my Savior.

There was so much brokenness in my life, and I would never have gone to God in my brokenness without someone leading me there. It was my community who circled me with love, support and encouragement that helped me find the strength to stand. It was my community who, accepting everything that I was, everything that I thought, everything that I felt, helped me find the strength to ask God for help. It was my community who showed me the love of Jesus, which helped me seek healing and restoration. When I sought it, God was more than willing.

The God of Restoration can restore anything that has been lost and broken. He restored my hardened heart so I could accept His love and give of my love. He restored my mind by lifting the veil of negativity. He restored my life through the cross and helped me to claim that forgiveness. It was at the point where I was completely surrendered and bare that restoration became mine. And when I allowed Him to restore me, that was when I could arise.

> **The God of Restoration doesn't do things half-heartedly.**

Take His hand and He will restore what was taken from you. And when He does, He will help you rise.

chapter fifteen

CLOSING DECLARATION

And now, arise Daughter. Arise Son. Come as you are and arise to the glory of the God of love, of mercy, of restoration. Arise and let His healing grace flow over you from the top of your head to the soles of your feet. May His anointing overtake the deepest, darkest part of you. May He restore to you all that He has promised. May He cradle you in His arms as He heals every tender piece of your heart, every broken promise, every trauma laced fear.

Hear Him as He calls out your name. Son! Daughter! My beloved. God has chosen you. You are not an accident. You are His. Your past does not define you. Jesus does. He defines all that you are, all that you mean to Him. Do not let guilt, self-condemnation, or self-hatred overtake you and consume you. Arise, run into our Father's open arms.

Allow Him to gently rock you. Allow Him to bring comfort to your tired spirit. May you feel the burden of your pain lifted from your shoulders. God sees how hard you try to handle your heart. He is asking you to trust Him and cry out to Him. He knows your pain. Cry out to Him and find freedom. Arise, return to Him and claim your inheritance.

May God heal you. May He heal you from all physical ailments. May He heal you from the torture in your mind. May He heal you from the affliction of other people's opinions of you, and the opinions you have chosen to believe. May God touch your heart and make you tender to yourself. Let go of the part of your heart that only He can heal. Now arise and be made whole.

xoxo

APPENDIX A
RESOURCES

The traumas retold in this book can be really heavy, especially for those who have experienced a similar event. Resources are available if you find yourself in a situation where you are feeling lost and alone. Your city and state will have resources as well.

If you or someone you know are in immediate danger, please call 911.

The Crisis Text Line is available Nationwide. Text HOME to 741741 to reach a Crisis Counselor. You can also go to their website at www.crisistextline.org

Sexual Assault Resources

Every state has a Rape Crisis line available 24 hours a day. For Washington you can go to the WCSAP site and choose the city or county near you and find a counselor, support group or help near you. www.wcsap.org/help/csap-by-city

National Crisis Line – 866-427-4747

RAINN (Rape, Abuse & Incest National Network) – provided victims of sexual assault with free, confidential services around the clock.
Phone: 1-800-656-HOPE
Web: www.rainn.org

Love is Respect – resources for teen dating abuse.
Phone: 866-331-9474
Text: text the phrase LOVEIS to 22522
www.loveisrespect.org

Child Abuse Resources

Adult Survivors of Child Abuse – supports survivors to heal and move on with their lives.
Email: info@ascasupport.org
Phone: 415-928-4576
Web: www.ascasupport.org

Childhelp – dedicated to helping victims of child abuse and neglect.
Phone: 800-4 A CHILD
Web: www.childhelp.org

The Blue Ribbon Project – community resource for child abuse victims and survivors.
Phone: 800-757-8120
Web: blueribbonproject.org

Suicide Resources

National Suicide Prevention Lifeline – free and confidential support 24/7 for people in distress.
Phone: 800-273-8255
Web: suicidepreventionlifeline.org

American Foundation for Suicide Prevention – provides resources for suicide prevention for you or someone you know.
Web: www.afsp.org

Mental Health

Washington Recovery HelpLine – provides free and confidential support 24/7 for people in distress.
Phone: 866-789-1511 (call or text)
Web: www.warecoveryhelpline.org

SAMHSA – (Substance Abuse and Mental Health Services) provides free and confidential around the clock support for you or a loved one.
Phone: 800-662-HELP
Web: www.samhsa.gov/find-help/national-helpline

National Eating Disorder Hotline – provides free and confidential support for you or a loved one. Free chat option is available online.
Phone: 800-931-2237
Web: www.nationaleatingdisorders.org/help-support/contact-helpline

APPENDIX B
LOSS HISTORY GRAPH

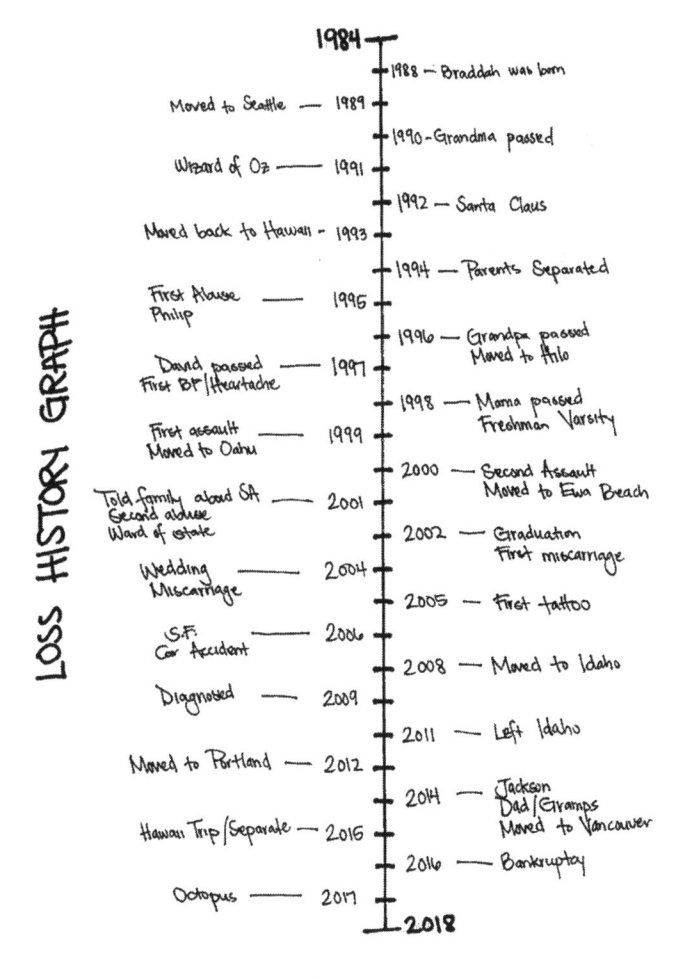

LOSS HISTORY GRAPH

- 1984
- 1988 — Braddah was born
- Moved to Seattle — 1989
- 1990 — Grandma passed
- Wizard of Oz — 1991
- 1992 — Santa Claus
- Moved back to Hawaii — 1993
- 1994 — Parents Separated
- First Abuse Philip — 1995
- 1996 — Grandpa passed / Moved to Hilo
- David passed / First BF/Heartache — 1997
- 1998 — Mama passed / Freshman Varsity
- First assault / Moved to Oahu — 1999
- 2000 — Second Assault / Moved to Ewa Beach
- Told family about SA / Second abuse / Ward of estate — 2001
- 2002 — Graduation / First miscarriage
- Wedding / Miscarriage — 2004
- 2005 — First tattoo
- SF / Car Accident — 2006
- 2008 — Moved to Idaho
- Diagnosed — 2009
- 2011 — Left Idaho
- Moved to Portland — 2012
- 2014 — Jackson / Dad/Gramps / Moved to Vancouver
- Hawaii Trip/Separate — 2015
- 2016 — Bankruptcy
- Octopus — 2017
- 2018

APPENDIX C
RELATIONSHIP GRAPH

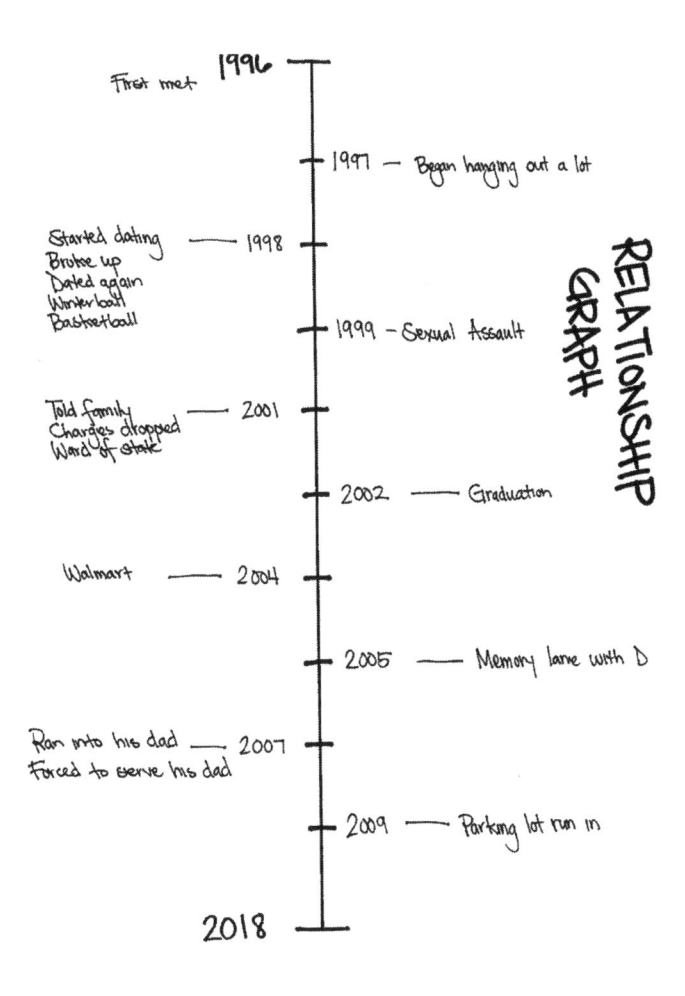

1996 — First met

1997 — Began hanging out a lot

1998
- Started dating
- Broke up
- Dated again
- Winterball
- Basketball

1999 — Sexual Assault

2001
- Told family
- Charges dropped
- Ward of state

2002 — Graduation

2004 — Walmart

2005 — Memory lane with D

2007
- Ran into his dad
- Forced to serve his dad

2009 — Parking lot run in

2018

RELATIONSHIP GRAPH

APPENDIX D
RECOVERY COMPONENTS

In your Recovery Components you will write down Amends, Forgiveness or Significant Emotional Statements for every event on your relationship graph.

- **Amends** (things you need to make amends for)

- **Forgiveness** (things you need to forgive)

- **Significant Emotional Statements**–SES (things you didn't need to amend or forgive but want to say)

1996 – First met.

    SES – I trusted you.
        We became friends.

1997 – We began to hang out.

1998 – We started dating.

    SES – I thought you were into my best friend. You made me feel special when you took my hand.

1998 – Broke up.

> **F** – I forgive you for lying.
> **A** – I'm sorry I was so angry.
>
> **SES** – I wish I knew then you weren't good for me.
> I trusted you.

1998 – Dating Again.

> **F** – I forgive you for lying.

1998 – Winter Ball

> **SES** – We had fun dancing.
> We laughed and smiled all night.

1999 – Sexual Assault.

> **F** – I forgive you for taking my innocence.
> I forgive you for breaking my trust.
> I forgive you for hurting me.
> I forgive you for raping me.
>
> **SES** – I trusted you.
> I hated you.
> I was ashamed of myself.
> I was afraid of you.
> I wanted to die.

2000 – Told my family.

> **A** – I am sorry I wasn't strong enough to come out earlier.
>
> **F** – I forgive you for denying it.
>
> **SES** – I hated you.
> I was afraid of you.
> I felt even more broken.

2002 – Graduating at a different school.

> **SES** – I felt alone in a school I barely knew anyone.

2004 – Walmart.

> **A** – I am sorry for giving you so much power.
>
> **SES** – I hated you.
> I was afraid of you.
> I have never felt so anxious in my life.
> I felt betrayed.
> I was ashamed of myself.
> I felt alone.

2005 – Walking down memory lane with an old friend

> **F** – I forgive you for causing me so much pain.
> I forgive you for the anxiety.

> **SES** – I was ashamed of myself.

2007 – Serving your Dad

> **F** – I forgive you for causing all this pain.
> I forgive you for lying.
> I forgive you for the anxiety.
> I forgive you for the depression.
> I forgive you for raping me.

> **SES** – I was ashamed of myself.
> I felt cornered.
> I felt trapped.
> I felt alone.

2009 – Run in with you in the parking lot

> **F** – I forgive you for causing me anxiety.

> **SES** – I felt cornered and trapped.

APPENDIX E
FORGIVENESS LETTER TO MR. POPULAR

In the letter I wrote to my sexual assaulter I called him by his name, which is why it has been omitted here. Using the items in your Recovery Components you write a letter to the person you want to release. Including their name for every Amends, Forgiveness and SES is important because it allows you to associate what you're saying to that person. For me, saying his name made me think of what I was saying and really mean it.

Dear _____,

I've been going through our relationship and there are a few things I want to say.

___, I'm sorry I wasn't strong enough to come out earlier.

___, I'm sorry for giving you so much power.

___, I forgive you for lying to me.

___, I forgive you for taking my innocence.

___, I forgive you for breaking my trust.

___, I forgive you for hurting me.

___, I forgive you for denying what you did to me.

___, I forgive you for causing all this pain.

___, I forgive you for the anxiety.

___, I forgive you for the depression.

___, I forgive you for raping me.

___, I want you to know that I trusted you. We became friends and you always made me laugh. Made me feel special. Every time you took my hand, I believed you cared.

___, I want you to know that I wish I knew then that you weren't good for me. Even when we danced. And laughed through the night. Or played basketball and practiced together.

___, I want you to know I hated you. I was afraid of you. But I don't hate you anymore. I know there is nothing to fear.

___, I want you to know I was ashamed of myself for what you did. I wanted to die. I felt so broken when it happened and more broken when I came out.

___, I want you to know I felt betrayed by you. You left me lonely. I felt so alone. I felt cornered and trapped.

___, I want you to know that I'm determined to ensure that other people don't feel as alone as I did going through an assault. I will write poems. I will write books. I will write blogs. I will use the voice I have been given to let them know they aren't alone and to stand together to become survivors and warriors. Not victims.

___, I want you to know you did not win.

Goodbye, _____.

APPENDIX F
FORGIVENESS LETTER TO MYSELF

Dear Pearl,

You and I have been through so much together. I think it's time we have this conversation.

Pearl, I'm sorry you felt you had to protect yourself.

Pearl, I'm sorry for believing the lies of others.

Pearl, I'm sorry for believing that ending your life was an option.

Pearl, I'm sorry you felt so alone and unwanted.

Pearl, I'm sorry thinking hiding the sexual assault would protect yourself and those you loved.

Pearl, I'm sorry you felt you could never be anything good.

Pearl, I'm sorry you couldn't trust people, that you thought they would hurt you.

Pearl, I'm sorry for the belief that you are broken, that you are weak.

Pearl, I forgive you for the years you've spent hating yourself.

Pearl, I forgive you for the forced *palu-ing*.

Pearl, I forgive you for the cutting.

Pearl, I forgive you for the burning.

Pearl, I forgive you for the alcohol and drug use.

Pearl, I forgive you for putting your walls up.

Pearl, I forgive you for pushing people away who could help you. I understand why you did.

Pearl, I forgive you for finding solace away from God.

Pearl, I want you to know the child abuse wasn't your fault.

Pearl, I want you to know the sexual abuse wasn't your fault.

Pearl, I want you to know the infertility and loss of your babies isn't your fault.

Pearl, you have a beautiful heart that is unselfish, incredibly loyal and full of love.

CLOSING DECLARATION

Pearl, you have a chosen family who stands beside you in every bump in the road, every success. Encouraging you to soar.

Pearl, I want you to know you are good, you're not a rotten apple.

Pearl, you are incredibly loved. You are wanted.

Pearl, I want you to know you are an inspiration. You encourage others, love on others to be the very best versions of themselves.

Pearl, remember Psalm 27:5 "For in the day of trouble he will keep me safe in his dwelling; he will hide me in the shelter of his sacred tent and set me high upon a rock." Not only will He be there in your time of troubles He will CARRY you.

Pearl, I want you to know you were not a mistake. That God didn't accidentally choose you. You weren't the last person on the team to be chosen.

Pearl means STRONG.

Always,

Me

ACKNOWLEDGMENTS

When I dreamt of this book I didn't envision all the people along the way that would make this a reality. This book could not have been made possible without the following people. All of my love and appreciation to you.

- My husband, Jeremy – Your belief and encouragement kept me going. Thank you for your love, patience and taking care of our sweet babies.
- Katie Law and Ashley Vanderpool – You have been by my side through the good and the bad encouraging me, lifting me up in prayer and being my sounding board.
- Nikki Ryll – for your photography expertise and making me feel comfortable in my skin.
- Dr. Brian Davenport and Pastor Laura Davenport – Your stewardship and your love for Jesus has inspired me to cultivate my relationship with Jesus.

- Pastor Callie Shipp Gray – for your obedience to pray and call for the Mothers of Zion.
- Pastor Jenny Donnelly and Tetelestai Ministries – For your servanthood and selflessness, you all show to the people in the Pacific Northwest and beyond.
- Jessie Schultz – For being the thumb in my back pushing me to bring this project to fruition.
- David Sluka – For the teaching and support you provided on a beautiful weekend in Oregon.
- Lisa McColm and Carol Law – For the hours poured in to edit my heart on these pages.
- Yvonne Parks at PearCreative.ca – For a beautiful cover and expertise to calm my newbie-ness.
- My dear friends Jasmine Schmidt, Shannon Marshall Pierce, Laurie Sperry, Julianne Kirkland and Gina Peak who took the time to do a peer review of this project.
- To all of you who are a part of Writer's Voice for your encouragement, support and prayers.

ABOUT THE AUTHOR

Pearl Flores is a mother, an author, a blogger and lifelong learner. Born and raised in Honolulu, Hawaii she brings a small town island twist of hard work, loyalty and aloha to her life on the mainland. She and her husband, Jeremy, have felt called to become foster parents loving the children of a vulnerable population. Pearl's passion to help find the voice for the voiceless has helped her become an advocate for these children, helping them to find a sanctuary in her home in the Pacific Northwest.

Made in the USA
Columbia, SC
11 February 2023